Taste of Home
Gifts FROM THE
Country
Kitchen

A TASTE OF HOME/READER'S DIGEST BOOK

Editor: Jennifer Olski
Associate Editor: Janet Briggs
Art Director: Kathy Crawford
Proofreader: Jean Steiner
Editorial Assistant: Barb Czysz
Food Editor: Janaan Cunningham
Senior Recipe Editor: Sue A. Jurack
Food Photography: Reiman Photo Studio

Executive Editor/Books: Heidi Reuter Lloyd
Senior Editor/Retail Books: Jennifer Olski
Creative Director: Ardyth Cope
Senior Vice President/Editor in Chief: Catherine Cassidy
President: Barbara Newton
Founder: Roy Reiman

Pictured on front cover:
Crispy Peanut Buter Balls (p. 14); Cranberry Chocolate Chip Cookie Mix (p. 19).

International Standard Book Number (10): 0-89821-710-5
International Standard Book Number (13): 978-0-89821-710-0
Library of Congress Control Number: 2008936666

For other Taste of Home books and products, visit www.tasteofhome.com.

For more Reader's Digest products and information,
visit www.rd.com (in the United States)
www.rd.ca (in Canada)

Printed in USA
1 3 5 7 9 10 8 6 4 2

Contents

Give a Gift of Good Taste from Your Kitchen

Whip up a batch of gooey chocolate brownies for your coworkers or throw together a hearty casserole for a dear friend…and watch them grin with delight at your tasty gift from the heart!

Whether you treat your new neighbors to a fresh batch of moist muffins for their housewarming or surprise a gracious hostess with a scrumptious cake, gifts of food prepared from scratch in your own kitchen are a special, personal way to show friends and family just how much they mean to you.

Selecting the Perfect Gift

When choosing a recipe to make for gift-giving, start by considering the special occasion for the gift or matching the recipe to the person's food and lifestyle interests.

For someone who's watching their sugar intake, skip the dessert and instead make a savory batch of Parmesan-Garlic Popcorn (page 163) for snacking. Invited to a holiday open house? Select a thank-you gift that everyone can enjoy; take along an assortment of Holiday Truffles (page 13).

When someone's feeling a bit under the weather, brighten their day with a crock of Comforting Chicken Noodle Soup (page 159) or a casserole of classic Fancy Mac 'n' Cheese (page 147).

And if you want to be prepared no matter what special event or gift-giving occasion pops up, plan ahead by preparing batches of pantry staples such as Spicy Mustard (page 177), Cinnamon Apple Jelly (page 180) or Mediterranean Herb Rub (page 181).

Wrapping It Up

Before you present your gift, take a few moments to create a label with the name. If you like, also jot out the entire recipe on a recipe card and attach it. Your friends will appreciate this thoughtful gesture, especially when they want to recreate the flavorful foods you've made for them!

For perishable items, be sure to include storage instructions, length of time your gift will keep and, if

appropriate, heating directions. For items like a meat rub or a sauce, give suggestions for use and include an extra recipe or two.

Now you're ready to package the gift! There are many fun, affordable and creative ways to wrap up your food gifts. During holiday seasons, craft stores sell a variety of papier-mache boxes. Pick out your favorites and decorate them with paint, rubber stamps, handmade papers or more. When you're finished, line the boxes with wax-coated tissue paper. (Wax-coated tissue paper can be found at specialty cooking stores. It's sturdier than regular tissue paper and won't absorb the cookie's flavors and oils.)

Decorative tins, plates, baskets, candy dishes and other serving pieces can often be found at bargain prices throughout the year at stores or at garage sales and Internet auctions. Keep a few on hand for last-minute gifts.

Also keep an eye open for boxes, bags and baskets to package your goodies. You can dress up kraft bags and boxes with ribbons, bows, raffia or strips of fabric. Cinch a plain plastic bag with a beaded foil twist and you'll have a classy fastener that also keeps your recipe card firmly attached.

For more crafty ideas on presenting your homemade treats, turn to page 6. But first, here are some quick wrap-ups for festive presentations:

Candies and cookies: Arrange them on a small plate or tray. Pack an assortment in tissue paper-lined boxes or tins. Stack them and wrap in plastic wrap or cellophane, then tie both ends with ribbon. For a more permanent gift, fill a cookie jar with cookies.

Cakes: Place layer cakes on a cake plate or stand and wrap cellophane around it and tie with a ribbon. For sheet cakes, make a special-occasion cake board. Cut a piece of foam core about 4 inches longer and 4 inches wider than the cake. Cover the foam board with wrapping paper, colored foil or cloth and attach to the bottom of the board with tape. Then cover the paper, foil or cloth with clear cellophane and attach to the bottom of the board.

Cheesecakes: Cut the cheesecake into individual slices. Place on mismatched dessert plates that you've found at flea markets or rummage sales. Wrap in cellophane and add a bow.

Chili: Place a container of chili in a large basket with soup mugs and rolls or crackers.

Coffee cakes: Cut the coffee cake into pieces and place on a snack tray with a coffee cup.

Ice cream toppings: Make a topping kit in a decorative box. Include the homemade topping, chopped nuts, a jar of maraschino cherries and a can of whipped cream.

Jams and jelly: Transfer the homemade jam or jelly into a glass jelly dish with a lid and spoon. Or, just make the jam or jelly jar a little more festive by covering the lid with cloth. The cloth can be tied onto the jar with string, ribbon or raffia.

Muffins or yeast rolls: Place in a napkin-lined basket with a pretty bow on the handle. Add some molded butter pats, a crock of flavored butter or a jar of honey. Muffins could also be placed in a new muffin pan and wrapped in cellophane.

Quick breads: Wrap in plastic wrap, then cover with a pretty kitchen towel and tie with ribbon.

Soup: Pour chilled soup into a heavy-duty resealable plastic bag, then place in a soup tureen. Tape lid down and add a bow.

Snack mixes: Place in a clear airtight canister or a large snack bowl.

Yeast bread: Wrap in plastic wrap, then tie to a cutting board with kitchen string, ribbon or raffia.

Shipping Gifts

If you're shipping food gifts, select items that will travel well. Perishable foods (those that need to be refrigerated or frozen) or fragile items like delicate cookies that can crumble or break easily are best hand-delivered to local friends and family. Good choices for shipping are firm cookies, bars, muffins, preserves, candies that won't easily melt, quick breads, pound cakes or fruitcakes. Always make sure the items are freshly baked, but completely cooled before packing and shipping. That will ensure the freshest and best possible gift will arrive at its destination.

Be sure to place foods in individual containers. To prevent breakage, crumple some waxed paper and place it around the food so that it is snug in the container. Wrap individual jars in several layers of newspaper.

For cookies, select ones that are sturdy and will travel well, such as drop, slice or sandwich cookies or bars and brownies. To help them stay fresh and intact, wrap them in bundles of two (for drop cookies, place their bottoms together) with plastic wrap. (See photos at right.)

Wrap bars individually. Pack crisp and soft cookies in separate tins and pack strong-flavored cookies such as gingersnaps, away from mild-flavored cookies. If the cookies do crumble during shipping, they'll make a tasty topping sprinkled over ice cream or a crunchy layer in a parfait.

Pack the food containers in sturdy shipping cartons. If packing multiple items, place the heavier ones on the bottom. Leave space around each container and cushion each with crumbled newspaper, bubble wrap or packing peanuts. Shake the shipping carton and fill to the top with the packing material so that the food containers cannot shift around.

If you do decide to ship an item that requires refrigeration, then follow these suggestions. First, arrange a delivery date with the recipient. That way they can at be home when the package arrives and can promptly place it in the refrigerator or freezer. Then, pack the cold or frozen food in foam shipping containers with frozen gel packs. Any empty space should be filled with crumpled paper or shipping peanuts to insulate the food and keep it cold or frozen. Next, label the package as "perishable" and "keep refrigerated" or "keep frozen." And most importantly, ship the package for next-day delivery.

Poinsettia Gift Bags and Package Tags —*Sharon Hoover, Bronson, Michigan*

Materials needed:

☐ Patterns on this page; ☐ tracing or pattern paper; ☐ pencil; ☐ 1 yard of 1/8-inch-wide green satin ribbon; ☐ size 24 tapestry needle; ☐ paintbrushes—small flat and liner; ☐ acrylic paint—bright red and green; ☐ palette or foam plate; ☐ permanent markers—extra fine-line gold metallic and fine-line black; ☐ tacky craft glue; ☐ gold glitter or gold glitter paint; ☐ ruler; ☐ scissors; ☐ decorative paper edger or pinking shears (optional); ☐ paper towels; ☐ scrap paper.
FOR THREE PACKAGE TAGS: ☐ One 8-1/2- x 11-inch piece of white typing paper.
FOR SMALL AND LARGE GIFT BAGS: ☐ Two white paper lunch bags.

Finished size: Folded package tags are about 2 inches x 2-1/2 inches, small gift bag is 7-3/4 inches tall and large gift bag is about 10-1/4 inches tall.

DIRECTIONS:

With fine-line black marker, trace patterns onto tracing paper as indicated on pattern. Place small amounts of each color paint on palette or foam plate as needed. Let paint dry thoroughly after each application.

PACKAGE TAGS:

1. Cut typing paper into three 2-1/4- x 5-1/2-inch pieces. Fold each in half, matching short edges. Open pieces and lay on flat surface.

2. Slip single poinsettia pattern underneath one tag, centering on one side of tag. Trace poinsettia onto tag with pencil. Repeat for remaining tags.

3. Using liner and red, outline each poinsettia petal on each tag. With small flat brush and red, fill in centers of petals.

4. Paint leaves green in the same manner.

5. Using gold metallic fine-line marker, outline petals and leaves and draw veins on leaves. Let dry.

6. Put a small dab of glue on center of each poinsettia and sprinkle with gold glitter or paint center with gold glitter paint. Let dry.

7. Fold and trim with decorative paper edger or pinking shears if desired.

8. Cut three 6-inch pieces of green ribbon. Thread tapestry needle with one piece and stitch ribbon through upper left corner of inside of one tag. Remove needle, center ribbon in hole and tie ends close to tag. Repeat for remaining tags.

SMALL GIFT BAG:

1. Cut 2 inches off top of one lunch bag. Measure 1 inch down from top of bag at inside of each corner and mark

PAINTING PATTERN
Trace one (entire pattern)—tracing paper
Trace one (smallest poinsettia only)—tracing paper

Note: For Package Tags, trace only smallest poinsettia and leaf.

For Large Gift Bag, flop traced pattern and retrace on back of tracing paper with marker so pattern will be reversed.

these points with pencil. Cut to pencil mark in each corner. Fold top of bag down 1 inch to inside of bag and glue folded edges into place.

2. Slide entire poinsettia pattern inside bag and position as shown in photo above, with ribbon ends about 1/2 inch from top and bottom edges of bag. Trace pattern onto bag.

3. Follow directions for painting tags to paint bag, making sure to slide a piece of scrap paper inside bag first to prevent paint from seeping through to back of bag. Draw outline of ribbon with gold metallic fine-line marker after painting is completed.

4. For handles, measure 1 inch in from each side and 1/2 inch down from the top edge of front and back of bag and mark with pencil.

5. Cut two 9-inch pieces of green ribbon. Thread one piece onto needle and knot one end. Insert needle from inside to outside of bag at mark on right side of front of bag and from outside to inside at mark on left side (see Fig. 1). Remove needle and tie a knot close to end of ribbon on inside of bag. Repeat for back of bag.

LARGE GIFT BAG:

1. Flop pattern, tracing on reverse side with black fineline marker. Slide retraced pattern inside bag, positioning as shown in photo, and trace pattern onto bag with a pencil. (Pattern will be reversed.)

2. Place a piece of scrap paper into bag to prevent paints from seeping through and paint as described for gift tags and small gift bag.

3. Trim top edges of white lunch bag with decorative paper edger or pinking shears if desired.

FIG. 1 Attaching ribbon handle

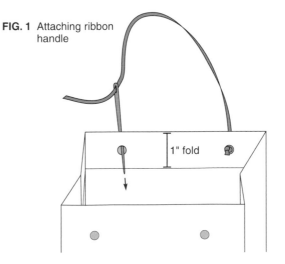

1" fold

Cookie Cutter Treat Bags —*Pat Childs, Tucson, Arizona*

Materials needed:

☐ Any metal or plastic cookie cutter of your choice; ☐ felt in color or colors that seem appropriate for the cookie cutter shape (i.e. white and red for candy canes, brown for a horse or teddy bear, green for a tree or wreath, tan for a gingerbread boy, etc.); ☐ 9- x 24-inch piece of a small coordinating Christmas print fabric with the 24-inch length cut on the straight of grain; ☐ matching or contrasting all-purpose thread; ☐ 18-1/2-inch length of any coordinating 1/2- to 1-inch-wide ribbon for the casing (bias tape can be substituted); ☐ 1 yard of thin jute string; ☐ embellishments of your choice to coordinate with the cookie cutter shape (i.e. yarn for horse's tail and reins, jingle bells, buttons, tiny pom-poms, sequins or beads to decorate a tree, wreath or gingerbread figure, etc.); ☐ recipe card; ☐ round paper hole punch; ☐ tacky craft glue (optional); ☐ safety pin; ☐ standard sewing supplies.

Finished size: Bags are 11-3/4 inches long x 8-1/2 inches wide. To adjust the size, begin with larger or smaller pieces of fabric.

DIRECTIONS FOR ONE:

APPLIQUES:

1. Lay the cookie cutter shape of your choice onto a piece of felt, choosing a color that suits the cutter, and trace around its shape. Cut out, removing traced lines as you cut.

2. Press under a 1/4-inch hem along each 9-inch edge of the 9- x 24-inch piece of Christmas print fabric.

3. With wrong sides together, fold this piece in half to form an 11-3/4- x 9-inch piece. Do not press in the fold.

4. Lay the felt shape on front of folded piece to decide on its position. If needed, add additional shapes to fill out the design. Decide on how the design will be embellished, trying different arrangements of craft items of your choice.

5. Remove any items that will get in the way when sewing the applique in place. Set aside to add later. Remove applique and sew or glue remaining embellishments onto felt as planned.

For example, 3/8-inch-wide strips of red felt were cut and laid out onto each candy cane shape on one of the bags shown in photo above right. The candy canes were then removed from the bag and the long edges of each stripe were sewn in place with red thread and a tiny straight stitch.

6. Return the felt shape or shapes to the front of the bag and pin in place through top layer of fabric only.

7. If any trims need to be tucked under the edges, pin trims in place.

For example, three colors of worsted-weight yarn were braided together for the tail of the horse on the other bag shown. One end was tucked under the back of the applique. Another braid was created for the reins. A jingle bell was added to the reins and the ends were tucked under the applique.

8. Unfold the bag and use either a matching or contrasting color thread and a tiny straight stitch to machine-sew around each felt shape, stitching close to the edge.

9. Sew or glue in place any embellishments that had been set aside earlier.

BAG:

All stitching is done with matching or coordinating thread, a medium straight stitch, a 1/4-inch seam allowance and a backstitch at beginning and end of seam.

1. Open up the pressed-under edges of the appliqued fabric. With right sides together, fold fabric in half so it measures 9 x 12 inches. Sew the 12-inch edges together on each side of bag.

2. Turn under the open edge along the pressed-in foldlines and stitch in place. Turn bag right side out and press.

3. Press under 1/2 inch at each end of ribbon. Turn bag so applique is on top. Beginning and ending at the seam on right-hand side of bag, pin ribbon right side up around bag about 1/8 to 1/4 inch from the top.

4. Sew the ribbon in place, stitching close to each long edge of ribbon. Leave short edges open.

5. Attach safety pin to one end of jute string. Use pin to pull the jute string through the casing.

6. Slip the cookie cutter onto one end of string and knot the end to keep it from falling off or tie end around cutter.

7. Write a recipe onto the recipe card if desired. Punch a hole in one corner of card. Pull remaining end of string through this hole and knot the end to keep it from falling off.

8. Tie on any other embellishments that coordinate with the design as desired.

Gifts from the Country Kitchen

Easter Egg Treat Box —*Debi Goldfisher, Wantagh, New York*

Materials needed:

☐ Pattern below right; ☐ tracing paper; ☐ pencil; ☐ scissors; ☐ 2-1/4-inch-high x 5-inch-wide round chipwood box; ☐ felt—one 4- x 6-inch scrap each of deep rose and yellow; ☐ six-strand embroidery floss to match each color of felt; ☐ embroidery needle; ☐ two 3-inch lengths of 3/8-inch-wide spring print ribbon; ☐ 1 yard of dusty rose 1/4-inch-wide satin picot ribbon; ☐ four assorted red and pink ribbon roses with leaves; ☐ polyester fiberfill; ☐ water basin; ☐ paper towels; ☐ foam plate; ☐ acrylic craft paints—dusty rose, light green and yellow; ☐ 1-inch foam paintbrush; ☐ small sea sponge (found where crafts or art supplies are sold); ☐ clear acrylic spray sealer; ☐ tacky craft glue; ☐ glue gun and glue stick; ☐ measuring tape; ☐ straight pins.

Finished size: Treat box is about 2-3/4 inches high x 5 inches wide.

DIRECTIONS:

EGGS:

1. Trace pattern onto tracing paper and cut out. Cut felt as directed on pattern.

2. Center a 3-inch length of spring print ribbon across the front of one yellow egg as shown on pattern. Pin in place. Fold the excess ribbon at each end to the back of egg and pin in place. With wrong sides together and edges even, pin second yellow egg in back. Prepare deep rose egg in same way.

3. Cut an 18-inch length of deep rose six-strand embroidery floss and separate the strands. Thread needle with two strands and knot the long end.

Blanket-stitch the edges of the yellow eggs together, hiding all knots on the inside and adding a small amount of fiberfill between the layers as you stitch.

4. In the same way, use two strands of yellow floss to blanket-stitch the edges of the deep rose egg. Remove pins.

BOX:

1. Paint outside of box and lid with two coats of yellow, letting paint dry between coats. Let dry.

2. Squeeze a small amount of dusty rose onto a paper plate. Dip a damp sea sponge into paint and blot off the excess on a paper towel. Lightly dab paint on all outside surfaces of box and lid. Let dry.

3. Dab outside of box and lid with light green in the same way.

4. When thoroughly dry, spray the box and lid with clear acrylic sealer following manufacturer's instructions. Let dry.

Assembly:

1. Measure across center and sides of lid and add 1/2 inch. Cut two pieces of picot ribbon equal to this length.

2. Use tacky glue to attach one ribbon piece across center of lid, folding the extra 1/4 inch at each end to the inside.

3. Center remaining piece across top of lid so ribbons cross, dividing lid into four equal parts. Glue as before.

4. Measure height of box without lid and add 1/2 inch. Cut four pieces of picot ribbon equal to this length.

5. Place lid on box to determine position of side ribbon pieces. Glue each side piece to outside of box, matching one cut end to the bottom edge of box and gluing the other end to inside of box.

6. Tie a bow with remaining picot ribbon and trim ends to desired length. Overlap the narrow ends of felt eggs and tack to center of bow with deep rose floss.

7. Referring to the photo for position, use the glue gun to attach four ribbon roses and the bow with eggs to the lid.

EGG
Trace 1—tracing paper
Cut 2—dusty rose felt
Cut 2—yellow felt

Ribbon placement

Halloween Treat Tins —*Dorlis Creager, Springtown, Texas*

Materials needed:

☐ Patterns below right; ☐ plastic-coated freezer paper; ☐ pencil; ☐ green and black fine-line permanent markers; ☐ scissors; ☐ ruler; ☐ masking tape; ☐ two empty 15-ounce vegetable or fruit cans; ☐ small hammer; ☐ awl; ☐ black and white spray paint; ☐ foam plate; ☐ acrylic craft paints—black, green, orange, white and yellow; ☐ kitchen sponge cut into 2-inch squares; ☐ 18-gauge craft wire; ☐ wire cutters; ☐ needle-nose pliers; ☐ raffia.

Finished size: Each can with handle is about 6-1/2 inches high x 3 inches wide.

DIRECTIONS:

1. Clean and dry cans. Turn each can on its side and lay it on a solid surface. Use the hammer to smooth any sharp edges on inside of can.

2. Use an awl to punch holes through opposite sides of each can 1/4 inch below the open edge. Use the hammer to flatten the edges around each hole.

PAINTING:

1. Spray-paint one can white and one can black. Let dry.

2. Put a dab of orange paint onto foam plate. Dip a damp sponge into the paint and dab the excess on a clean area of the plate. When most of the paint has been removed, lightly dab this color all over each can. Let dry.

3. On white can only, use another damp sponge to dab a little black over the orange paint in the same way. Let dry.

4. Cut two large pieces of freezer paper to fit around one side of each can between the punched holes. With shiny side down, center one piece on pumpkin pattern and the other piece on candy corn pattern. Trace the outline of each shape with pencil, including the eyes and mouth on the pumpkin.

5. Cut out each shape from the surrounding freezer paper to make stencils. Cut out the eyes and mouth from pumpkin cutout for a third stencil.

6. Tape the candy corn stencil onto the black can, centering the design between the punched holes on one side of can. Tape the larger stencil with the pumpkin shape onto the white can in the same way. (The piece with the eyes and mouth will be used later.)

7. Use a clean damp sponge to fill in the pumpkin and the bottom third of candy corn with orange.

8. Use another clean damp sponge and white to fill in the top third of the candy corn. Let dry.

9. Use a clean damp sponge and yellow to fill in the center third of the candy corn. When dry, remove stencils.

10. Position the pumpkin cutout with the eyes

and mouth on the stenciled pumpkin and sponge-paint the eyes and mouth green. Remove stencil and lightly dab green paint around the bottom of the pumpkin.

11. When white can is thoroughly dry, use the permanent markers to outline the pumpkin and add all remaining details as shown on pattern.

HANDLES:

1. Cut one 16-inch length of craft wire for each can. Wrap the center of each wire around a pencil five or six times to create coils. Remove pencil.

2. Poke one wire end through a hole on a can so the end comes out on the inside. Wrap this end around the pliers to create a loop that will hold the wire in place. Repeat with remaining end. Add handle to the other can in same way.

3. Tie a raffia bow around each wire handle. Trim raffia as desired.

CANDY CORN
Trace 1—dull side of freezer paper

PUMPKIN
Trace 1—dull side of freezer paper

Christmas

Spumoni Slices —Mary Chupp, Chattanooga, Tennessee

- 1 **cup butter, softened**
- 1-1/2 **cups confectioners' sugar**
- 1 **egg**
- 1 **teaspoon vanilla extract**
- 2-1/2 **cups all-purpose flour**
- 2 **squares (1 ounce** *each***) semisweet chocolate, melted**
- 1/2 **cup chopped pecans**
- 3 **to 5 drops green food coloring**
- 1/4 **cup finely chopped candied red cherries**
- 1/2 **teaspoon almond extract**
- 3 **to 5 drops red food coloring**

1. In a mixing bowl, cream butter and sugar. Beat in egg and vanilla. Gradually add flour and mix well. Divide the dough into three portions. Stir the chocolate into one portion; mix well. Add pecans and green food coloring to the second portion. Add the cherries, almond extract and red food coloring to the third.

2. Roll each portion between two pieces of waxed paper into an 8-in. x 6-in. rectangle. Remove waxed paper. Place chocolate rectangle on a piece of plastic wrap. Top with the green and pink rectangles; press together lightly. Wrap with plastic wrap and chill overnight. Cut chilled dough in half lengthwise. Return one rectangle to the refrigerator.

3. Cut remaining rectangle into 1/8-in. slices. Place 1 in. apart on ungreased baking sheets. Bake at 375° for 5-7 minutes or until set. Cool for 2 minutes before removing to wire racks. Repeat with remaining dough. **Yield:** about 7 dozen.

Christmas Eve Mice –*Margene Pons, West Valley City, Utah*

24 double-stuffed cream-filled chocolate
   sandwich cookies
1 cup (6 ounces) semisweet chocolate
   chips
2 teaspoons shortening
24 red maraschino cherries with stems,
   well drained
24 milk chocolate kisses
48 sliced almonds
1 small tube green decorative icing gel
1 small tube red decorative icing gel

1. Carefully twist cookies apart; set aside the halves with cream filling. Save plain halves for another use. In a microwave or heavy saucepan, melt chocolate chips and shortening; stir until smooth.

2. Holding each cherry by the stem, dip in melted chocolate, then press onto the bottom of a chocolate kiss. Place on the cream filling of cookie, with cherry stem extending beyond cookie

edge. For ears, place slivered almonds between the cherry and kiss. Refrigerate until set.

3. With green gel, pipe holly leaves on the cream. With red gel, pipe holly berries between leaves and pipe eyes on each chocolate kiss. Store in an airtight container at room temperature. **Yield:** 2 dozen.

Coconut Fruitcake Cookies –*Jolene Davis, Minden, Nevada*

3 cups chopped pecans
2-1/2 cups flaked coconut
1-1/4 cups chopped candied cherries
1-1/4 cups chopped candied pineapple
1 cup chopped dates
2 cups sweetened condensed milk

1. In a bowl, combine the first five ingredients. Stir in milk. Fill paper-lined miniature muffin cups two-thirds full.

2. Bake at 300° for 20-25 minutes or until golden brown. Cool for 10 minutes before removing from pans to waxed paper to cool completely. Let stand for 24 hours in an airtight container at room temperature before serving. **Yield:** 8 dozen.

Holiday Truffles —Jennifer Lipp, Laurel, Nebraska

3 packages (12 ounces *each*) semisweet chocolate chips, *divided*
2-1/4 cups sweetened condensed milk, *divided*
1/2 teaspoon orange extract
1/2 teaspoon peppermint extract
1/2 teaspoon almond extract
1-1/2 pounds white candy coating, melted
3/4 pound dark chocolate candy coating, melted
1/2 cup ground almonds

1. In a microwave-safe bowl, melt one package of chips. Add 3/4 cup milk; mix well. Stir in orange extract. Repeat twice, adding peppermint extract to one portion and almond extract to the other. Cover and chill for 45 minutes or until firm enough to shape into 1-in. balls. Place on three separate waxed paper-lined baking sheets. Chill for 1-2 hours or until firm.

2. Dip the orange-flavored truffles twice in white candy coating; place on waxed paper to harden.

Dip peppermint-flavored truffles in dark chocolate coating. Dip almond-flavored truffles in dark chocolate, then roll in ground almonds. If desired, drizzle white coating over peppermint truffles and dark chocolate coating over orange truffles. **Yield:** about 7 dozen.

Nutmeg Logs —Marjorie Gegelmann, Bismarck, North Dakota

1 cup butter, softened
3/4 cup sugar
1 egg
2 teaspoons vanilla extract
3 cups all-purpose flour
1-1/2 teaspoons ground nutmeg
1/4 teaspoon salt
Additional sugar

1. In a mixing bowl, cream butter and sugar until light and fluffy. Beat in egg and vanilla. Combine the flour, nutmeg and salt; gradually add to the creamed mixture. Cover and refrigerate for 1 hour or until firm.

2. On a sugared surface, shape 1/2 cupfuls of dough into 1/2-in.-thick logs. Cut logs into 2- to 2-1/2-in. pieces. Place 2 in. apart on ungreased baking sheets. Bake at 350° for 12-14 minutes or until lightly browned. Remove to wire racks to cool. **Yield:** about 5 dozen.

Eggnog Cutout Cookies —*Glenna Tooman, Boise, Idaho*

1/2 **cup butter, softened**
1 **cup sugar**
2 **eggs**
2 **tablespoons plus 1 teaspoon eggnog**
2-1/2 **cups all-purpose flour**
1/2 **teaspoon salt**
1/4 **teaspoon baking soda**
1/4 **teaspoon ground nutmeg**
ICING:
2 **cups confectioners' sugar**
1/4 **teaspoon ground nutmeg, optional**
4 **to 5 tablespoons eggnog**
Liquid *or* paste food coloring, optional

1. In a mixing bowl, cream butter and sugar. Beat in eggs. Stir in eggnog. Combine the flour, salt, baking soda and nutmeg; gradually add to creamed mixture. Cover and refrigerate for 1 hour or until easy to handle.

2. On a lightly floured surface, roll out dough to 1/8-in. thickness. Cut with floured 2-1/2-in. cookie cutters. Place 2 in. apart on greased baking sheets. Bake at 375° for 8-10 minutes or until edges begin to brown. Remove to wire racks to cool.

3. In a mixing bowl, beat confectioners' sugar, nutmeg if desired and enough eggnog to achieve icing consistency. Add food coloring if desired. Spread over cooled cookies; let dry. **Yield:** about 4 dozen.

Editor's Note: This recipe was tested with commercially prepared eggnog.

Crispy Peanut Butter Balls —*Liz David, St. Catherines, Ontario*

2 **cups creamy peanut butter**
1/2 **cup butter, softened**
3-3/4 **cups confectioners' sugar**
3 **cups crisp rice cereal**
4 **cups (24 ounces) semisweet chocolate chips**
1/4 **cup plus 1 teaspoon shortening, *divided***
1/3 **cup vanilla *or* white chips**

1. In a large mixing bowl, beat peanut butter and butter until blended; gradually beat in confectioners' sugar. Stir in cereal. Shape into 1-in. balls. Refrigerate until chilled.

2. In a large microwave-safe bowl, combine chocolate chips and 1/4 cup shortening. Microwave on high until chips are melted; stir until smooth. Dip balls into chocolate; place on a waxed paper-lined pan.

3. In a small microwave-safe bowl, combine vanilla chips and remaining shortening. Microwave at 70% power until melted; stir until smooth. Drizzle over candies. Refrigerate until set. **Yield:** 6 dozen.

Editor's Note: Reduced-fat or generic brands of peanut butter are not recommended for this recipe.

Snowballs –*Muriel White, Brampton, Ontario*

1/2 cup butter
1 can (14 ounces) sweetened condensed milk
3 tablespoons baking cocoa
1 teaspoon vanilla extract
2 cups graham cracker crumbs (about 32 squares)
3-1/2 cups flaked coconut, *divided*
About 36 large marshmallows

1. Line a baking sheet with waxed paper; set aside. In a saucepan, combine the butter, milk, cocoa and vanilla. Cook and stir over medium heat until butter is melted and mixture is smooth. Remove from the heat; stir in cracker crumbs and 1-1/2 cups coconut. Let stand until cool enough to handle.

2. Using moistened hands, wrap about 1 tablespoon of mixture around each marshmallow (dip hands in water often to prevent sticking). Roll in remaining coconut; place on prepared baking sheet. Cover and freeze until firm. Store in an airtight container in the refrigerator or freezer. May be frozen for up to 2 months. **Yield:** about 3 dozen.

Peppermint Stick Sauce –*Linda Gronewaller, Hutchinson, Kansas*

1-1/2 cups finely crushed peppermint candies *or* candy canes
3/4 cup heavy whipping cream
1 jar (7 ounces) marshmallow creme

Combine all ingredients in a medium saucepan. Cook over medium-low heat, stirring occasionally, until mixture is smooth and candy is melted. Pour into small airtight containers. Store in the refrigerator. Serve warm over ice cream or cake. **Yield:** 3 cups.

Fruit-Filled Chocolate Container —*Taste of Home Test Kitchen*

16 squares (1 ounce *each*) semisweet chocolate
2 tablespoons shortening
2-1/2 ounces white candy coating
1 tablespoon light corn syrup
CHOCOLATE-DIPPED STRAWBERRIES:
24 squares (1 ounce *each*) semisweet chocolate
5 teaspoons shortening
1-1/2 teaspoons almond extract
5 dozen large fresh strawberries (about 2-1/2 quarts)

1. Line a 9-in. round baking pan with aluminum foil; set aside. In a heavy saucepan over low heat, melt chocolate and shortening; stir until smooth. Pour 3/4 cup into prepared pan; chill for 10 minutes or until firm. Spread a thin coating of the remaining melted chocolate around sides of pan (see photo 1 below); chill for 5 minutes. Continue coating until all of the melted chocolate has been used.

2. Break white candy coating into chunks; place in a microwave-safe bowl. Microwave at 70% power for 1 minute; stir. Microwave in 10-second intervals or until melted; stir until smooth. Add corn syrup; stir until mixture is thick. Pour onto waxed paper; press to 1/2-in. thickness. Let stand for 15-20 minutes or until easy to handle. Set aside 1 teaspoon for assembly.

3. Divide remaining coating into six equal portions. Roll each into a 15-in. rope. Press three rope ends together; braid and press end to secure. Repeat with remaining ropes. Set aside both braids.

4. For Chocolate-Dipped Strawberries: Melt chocolate and shortening in a microwave or heavy saucepan. Stir in almond extract. Dip strawberries halfway, allowing excess to drip off. Place on a waxed paper-lined tray; refrigerate for 30 minutes or until set.

5. To assemble, carefully remove chocolate container from pan by slowly pulling up on foil lining (see photo 2). Peel foil to remove.

6. Place small dabs of reserved white coating around top edge of container to secure the braids (see photo 3). Press one braid around half of container. Repeat with other braid; trim to fit if necessary. Cover and refrigerate until serving. Fill with chocolate-dipped berries. **Yield:** 1 chocolate container and about 2-1/2 dozen berries.

Making the Container

Photo 1. Using a small spatula, spread a thin, even coat of the remaining chocolate around the sides of pan. Chill for 5 minutes. Repeat until there is no more chocolate remaining.

Photo 2. Carefully remove your chocolate container from the pan, using the foil lining to lift it out. Invert container carefully onto a flat surface. Then gently peel off the foil.

Photo 3. Place small dollops of the reserved coating mixture around the top edge of the container. Carefully place the braid around the same edge and press down gently to secure.

Candy-Coated Tips for Trimming

• To add a special Christmas touch to this chocolate container, melt a little extra white candy coating. Divide into two equal portions, adding red paste or gel food coloring to one portion and green to the other. Roll coating to 1/4-inch thickness and cut with 1-inch cookie cutters into shapes such as holly leaves and berries or snowflakes. Attach cutout shapes to sides of container with a dab of melted chocolate.

• To give your strawberries an extra-festive look, crush some red and green hard mint candies. After dipping berries in melted chocolate, roll some of the berries in the crushed candies and place on waxed paper until dry. Decorate some with green, some with red and some with both colors. Or drizzle a little melted white candy coating in fun patterns over the chocolate-dipped end of each fruit.

Jolly Jelly Doughnuts —*Lee Bremson, Kansas City, Missouri*

2 packages (1/4 ounce *each*) active dry yeast
2 cups warm milk (110° to 115°)
7 cups all-purpose flour, *divided*
4 egg yolks
1 egg
1/2 cup sugar
1 teaspoon salt
2 teaspoons grated lemon peel
1/2 teaspoon vanilla extract
1/2 cup butter, melted
Oil for deep-fat frying
Red jelly of your choice
Additional sugar

1. In a large mixing bowl, dissolve yeast in warm milk. Add 2 cups flour; mix well. Let stand in a warm place for 30 minutes. Add the egg yolks, egg, sugar, salt, lemon peel and vanilla; mix well. Beat in butter and remaining flour. Do not knead. Cover and let rise in a warm place until doubled, about 45 minutes.

2. Punch dough down. On a lightly floured surface, roll out to 1/2-in. thickness. Cut with a 2-1/2-in. biscuit cutter. Place on lightly greased baking sheets. Cover and let rise until nearly doubled, about 35 minutes.

3. In a deep-fat fryer or electric skillet, heat oil to 375°. Fry doughnuts, a few at a time, for 1-1/2 to 2 minutes on each side or until browned. Drain on paper towels. Cool for 2-3 minutes; cut a small slit with a sharp knife on one side of each doughnut. Using a pastry bag with a small round tip or a small spoon, fill each doughnut with about 1 teaspoon jelly. Carefully roll doughnuts in sugar. Serve warm. **Yield:** about 2-1/2 dozen.

Miniature Fruitcakes —*Ruth Burrus, Zionsville, Indiana*

3/4 cup sugar
1/4 cup all-purpose flour
1/2 teaspoon baking powder
1/8 teaspoon salt
1-1/2 cups chopped walnuts
1 cup chopped dates
3/4 cup chopped mixed candied fruit (about 4 ounces)
2 eggs, *separated*
1/2 teaspoon vanilla extract
Halved candied cherries

1. In a bowl, combine the first seven ingredients. Combine egg yolks and vanilla; stir into dry ingredients. In a small mixing bowl, beat egg whites until stiff peaks form; fold into batter.

2. Fill greased and floured muffin cups two-thirds full. Cover muffin tin tightly with heavy-duty aluminum foil. Bake at 275° for 1 hour. Uncover; top with cherries. Bake 5 minutes longer or until a toothpick inserted near the center comes out clean. Cool for 5 minutes. Run a knife around the edges of each cup; remove to a wire rack to cool completely. **Yield:** 1 dozen.

Cranberry-Chocolate Chip Cookie Mix —*Shelley Friesen, Leduc, Alberta*

1-1/4 cups all-purpose flour
 1 teaspoon baking soda
 1/2 teaspoon salt
 1/2 teaspoon ground cinnamon
 3/4 cup packed brown sugar
 1 cup (6 ounces) semisweet chocolate chips
 1/2 cup dried cranberries
 1/2 cup chopped walnuts
 1/2 cup quick-cooking oats
ADDITIONAL INGREDIENTS:
 2/3 cup butter, softened
 1 egg
 3/4 teaspoon vanilla extract

1. In a small bowl, combine the flour, baking soda, salt and cinnamon. In a 1-qt. glass container, layer the flour mixture, brown sugar, 1/2 cup chocolate chips, cranberries, walnuts, oats and remaining chips. Cover and store in a cool dry place for up to 6 months. **Yield:** 1 batch (about 4 cups total)

2. To prepare the cookies: In a large mixing bowl, beat the butter, egg and vanilla until blended. Add cookie mix and mix well. Drop by rounded tablespoonfuls 2 in. apart onto ungreased baking sheets. Bake at 350° for 10-15 minutes or until golden brown. Remove to wire racks. **Yield:** 2-1/2 dozen.

Holiday Biscotti —*Libia Foglesong, San Bruno, California*

1/2 cup butter, softened
 1 cup sugar
 3 eggs
 2 teaspoons vanilla extract
 1 teaspoon orange extract
 3 cups all-purpose flour
 2 teaspoons baking powder
1/2 teaspoon salt
2/3 cup dried cranberries, coarsely chopped
2/3 cup pistachios, coarsely chopped
 2 tablespoons grated orange peel

1. In a mixing bowl, cream butter and sugar. Add eggs, one at a time, beating well after each addition. Stir in extracts. Combine flour, baking powder and salt; gradually add to creamed mixture and mix well (dough will be sticky). Stir in cranberries, pistachios and orange peel. Chill for 30 minutes.

2. Divide dough in half. On a floured surface, shape each half into a loaf 1-1/2 to 2 in. in diameter. Place on an ungreased baking sheet. Bake at 350° for 30-35 minutes. Cool for 5 minutes.

3. Cut diagonally with a serrated knife into 3/4-in.-thick slices. Place slices cut side down on an ungreased baking sheet. Bake 9-10 minutes. Turn slices over. Bake 10 minutes more or until golden. Cool on a wire rack. Store in an airtight container. **Yield:** 2 dozen.

Christmas Hard Candy —*Jane Holman, Moultrie, Georgia*

3-1/2 cups sugar
1 cup light corn syrup
1 cup water
1/4 to 1/2 teaspoon cinnamon *or* peppermint oil
1 teaspoon red *or* green food coloring

1. In a large heavy saucepan, combine sugar, corn syrup and water. Cook on medium-high heat until candy thermometer reads 300° (hard-crack stage), stirring occasionally.

2. Remove from the heat; stir in oil and food coloring, keeping face away from mixture as odor is very strong. Immediately pour onto a baking sheet coated with nonstick cooking spray. Cool; break into pieces. Store in airtight containers. **Yield:** about 2 pounds.

Editor's Note: Cinnamon oil and peppermint oil are available in cake-decorating and candy supply stores. We recommend that you test your candy thermometer before each use by bringing water to a boil; the thermometer should read 212°. Adjust your recipe temperature up or down based on your test.

Eggnog Fruit Bread —*Margo Stich, Rochester, Minnesota*

3 eggs
1-1/2 cups eggnog
1 cup vegetable oil
1-1/2 cups sugar
3/4 teaspoon vanilla extract
3/4 teaspoon rum extract
3 cups all-purpose flour, *divided*
2 teaspoons baking powder
1/2 teaspoon salt
1/2 teaspoon ground nutmeg
1 cup candied fruit
1/2 cup chopped walnuts

1. In a mixing bowl, beat the eggs, eggnog and oil. Add the sugar and extracts; mix well. Combine 2-1/2 cups flour, baking powder, salt and nutmeg; gradually add to egg mixture. Toss the fruit with remaining flour; stir into batter. Fold in walnuts.

2. Pour into two greased 8-in. x 4-in. x 2-in. loaf pans. Bake at 350° for 60-65 minutes or until a toothpick inserted near the center comes out clean. Cool for 10 minutes before removing from pans to wire racks. **Yield:** 2 loaves.

Editor's Note: This recipe was tested with commercially prepared eggnog.

Chocolate Yule Log —*Bernadette Colvin, Houston, Texas*

4 eggs, *separated*
2/3 cup sugar, *divided*
1/2 cup all-purpose flour
2 tablespoons baking cocoa
1 teaspoon baking powder
1/4 teaspoon salt

FILLING:
1 cup heavy whipping cream
2 tablespoons sugar
1/4 teaspoon almond extract

FROSTING:
1/2 cup butter, softened
2 cups confectioners' sugar
2 squares (1 ounce *each*) unsweetened chocolate, melted
2 tablespoons milk
2 teaspoons vanilla extract

1. Line a greased 15-in. x 10-in. x 1-in. baking pan with waxed paper; grease the paper and set aside. In a mixing bowl, beat egg yolks until light and fluffy. Gradually add 1/3 cup sugar, beating until light and lemon-colored, about 5 minutes. In another mixing bowl, beat egg whites until foamy. Gradually add remaining sugar, beating until stiff peaks form. Fold into egg yolks, a third at a time. Combine the flour, cocoa, baking powder and salt; fold into egg mixture, a third at a time.

2. Spread batter into prepared pan. Bake at 375° for 10-12 minutes or until cake springs back when lightly touched. Cool for 5 minutes. Turn cake onto a kitchen towel dusted with confectioners' sugar. Gently peel off waxed paper. Roll up cake in the towel jelly-roll style, starting with a short side; cool completely on a wire rack.

3. Meanwhile, for the filling, beat the cream in a mixing bowl until thickened. Add the sugar and the almond extract, beating until almost stiff. Unroll the cake; spread the filling to within 1 in. of edges. Reroll cake.

4. In a mixing bowl, cream the butter and confectioners' sugar. Beat in the chocolate, milk and vanilla until smooth. Frost the cake, using a metal spatula to create a bark-like effect. **Yield:** 14-16 servings.

Peanut Candy Popcorn Balls —*Alida Jaeger, Ixonia, Wisconsin*

4 quarts popped popcorn
1-1/2 cups salted peanuts
1-1/2 cups chopped pecans
1 package (16 ounces) green and red milk chocolate M&M's
1/2 cup butter
1/2 cup vegetable oil
1 package (16 ounces) miniature marshmallows

1. In a large bowl, combine the popcorn, peanuts, pecans and M&M's; set aside. In a large saucepan, combine the butter, oil and marshmallows; cook and stir until smooth. Pour over popcorn mixture; mix well.

2. When cool enough to handle, shape into popcorn balls. Let stand at room temperature until firm before wrapping in plastic wrap or stacking. **Yield:** about 20 popcorn balls.

Gift of the Magi Bread —*Sandra Bonow, Lewiston, Minnesota*

1/2 cup butter, softened
1 cup sugar
2 eggs
1 teaspoon vanilla extract
2 cups all-purpose flour
1 teaspoon baking soda
1/2 teaspoon salt
1 cup mashed ripe bananas (about 2 medium)
1 can (11 ounces) mandarin oranges, drained
1 cup flaked coconut
1 cup (6 ounces) semisweet chocolate chips
2/3 cup sliced almonds, *divided*
1/2 cup chopped maraschino cherries
1/2 cup chopped dates

1. In a mixing bowl, cream butter and sugar. Beat in eggs and vanilla. Combine the flour, baking soda and salt; add to the creamed mixture alternately with bananas. Stir in the oranges, coconut, chocolate chips, 1/2 cup almonds, cherries and dates.

2. Pour into two greased 8-in. x 4-in. x 2-in. loaf pans. Sprinkle with remaining almonds. Bake at 350° for 50-55 minutes or until a toothpick inserted near the center comes out clean. Cool for 10 minutes before removing from pans to wire racks to cool completely. **Yield:** 2 loaves.

Easter

Lemon Ricotta Cheesecake –*Julie Nitschke, Stowe, Vermont*

1-1/2 cups vanilla wafer crumbs (about 45 wafers)
1/4 cup butter, melted
1 teaspoon grated lemon peel
FILLING:
2 packages (8 ounces *each*) cream cheese, softened
1 carton (15 ounces) ricotta cheese
1-1/4 cups sugar
1/4 cup cornstarch
4 eggs
2 cups half-and-half cream
1/3 cup lemon juice
3 teaspoons grated lemon peel
2 teaspoons vanilla extract
Fresh mint and lemon slices, optional

1. In a bowl, combine wafer crumbs, butter and lemon peel. Press onto the bottom of a greased 9-in. springform pan. Bake at 325° for 12-14 minutes or until lightly browned. Cool.

2. In a large mixing bowl, beat cream cheese and ricotta until smooth. Combine sugar and cornstarch; add to cheese mixture and beat well. Add eggs and cream, beating on low speed just until combined. Beat in lemon juice, peel and vanilla just until blended. Pour into crust. Place pan on a baking sheet.

3. Bake at 325° for 70-80 minutes or until center is almost set. Cool on a wire rack for 10 minutes. Carefully run a knife around edge of pan to loosen; cool 1 hour longer. Refrigerate overnight. Remove sides of pan. Garnish with mint and lemon if desired. **Yield:** 12-14 servings.

Strawberry Cheese Bundles —*Jolene Spray, Van Wert, Ohio*

1 package (3 ounces) cream cheese, softened
2 tablespoons confectioners' sugar
1/4 teaspoon almond extract
1 tube (8 ounces) refrigerated crescent rolls
1/3 cup strawberry pie filling
1/3 cup crushed pineapple, drained
2 to 3 tablespoons apricot spreadable fruit

1. In a small mixing bowl, beat the cream cheese, sugar and extract until smooth. Unroll crescent dough and separate into eight triangles. Place 1 heaping teaspoonful of cream cheese mixture in the center of each triangle. Top with 1 teaspoon of pie filling and 1 teaspoon of pineapple.

2. With one long side of pastry facing you, fold right and left corners over filling to top corner, forming a square. Seal edges. Place on an ungreased baking sheet. Bake at 375° for 15-17 minutes or until lightly browned. Brush with spreadable fruit. Serve warm or cold. **Yield:** 8 servings.

Cream Cheese Clouds —*Mary Ann Marino, West Pittsburgh, Pennsylvania*

1 package (8 ounces) cream cheese, softened
3/4 cup confectioners' sugar
1/2 teaspoon vanilla extract
1 cup heavy whipping cream
2 quarts fresh strawberries, sliced
1 carton (8 ounces) frozen whipped topping, thawed

1. In a mixing bowl, beat the cream cheese, sugar and vanilla until fluffy. Gradually add cream, beating until thickened. Spoon mixture into 10 mounds on a waxed paper-lined baking sheet. Using the back of a spoon, shape into 3-in. cups. Freeze for 2 hours or overnight.

2. To serve, fill with strawberries and garnish with whipped topping. **Yield:** 10 servings.

Easter Egg Sugar Cookies —Alison Benke, Chetwynd, British Columbia

1 cup butter, softened
1-1/4 cups sugar
3 eggs
1 teaspoon vanilla extract
1/2 teaspoon almond extract
3-1/2 cups all-purpose flour
1 teaspoon baking powder
1/2 teaspoon salt
ICING:
2 cups confectioners' sugar
1 tablespoon meringue powder
1/4 cup warm water
1/2 teaspoon almond extract
Liquid food coloring
Pastel organdy ribbon (1/4 inch wide), cut into 12-inch lengths, optional

1. In a mixing bowl, cream butter and sugar. Add eggs, one at a time, beating well after each addition. Add extracts. Combine the flour, baking powder and salt; gradually add to creamed mixture. Cover and refrigerate for 1 hour or until easy to handle.

2. On a lightly floured surface, roll out dough to 1/4-in. thickness. Cut with a 2-1/2-in. egg-shaped cookie cutter. Place 1 in. apart on lightly greased baking sheets. If desired, make a hole for a ribbon by pressing a plastic straw 1/2 in. from the top of each cookie. Bake at 375° for 8-10 minutes or until lightly browned. Remove to wire racks to cool.

3. For icing, sift confectioners' sugar and meringue powder into a mixing bowl. Add water and extract; beat on low speed until blended. Beat on high for 5 minutes. Fill a pastry or plastic bag with 1 cup of icing; cut a small hole in the corner of the bag. Outline each cookie with icing. Tint remaining icing with food coloring if desired. Add water, a few drops at a time, until mixture is thin enough to flow smoothly. Fill in the center space of each cookie, allowing the icing to spread to the outline. Let dry overnight.

4. Decorate with remaining icing. Store in airtight containers. If desired, thread ribbon through holes, tie ends in a bow and hang on an Easter tree. **Yield:** about 4-1/2 dozen.

Editor's Note: Meringue powder can be ordered by mail from Wilton Industries, Inc. Call 1-800/794-5866 or visit their Web site at www.wilton.com.

Orange Sour Cream Muffins —Mary Chupp, Chattanooga, Tennessee

1-1/4 cups all-purpose flour
1 cup sugar
1/2 cup chopped pecans
1/2 teaspoon baking soda
1/4 teaspoon salt
1 egg
1/2 cup sour cream
6 tablespoons butter, melted
3 tablespoons orange juice concentrate

1. In a bowl, combine the flour, sugar, pecans, baking soda and salt. In another bowl, whisk the egg, sour cream, butter and orange juice concentrate. Stir into the dry ingredients just until moistened.

2. Fill paper-lined muffin cups three-fourths full. Bake at 375° for 18-20 minutes or until a toothpick comes out clean. Cool for 5 minutes before removing from pans to a wire rack. Serve warm. **Yield:** 1 dozen.

Jelly Bean Brittle *–Kathy Kittel, Lenexa, Kansas*

    4 **tablespoons butter, *divided***
2-1/2 **cups miniature jelly beans**
    3 **cups sugar**
    1 **cup light corn syrup**
1/2 **cup water**
1/2 **teaspoon salt**
    2 **teaspoons baking soda**

1. In a microwave-safe bowl, melt 1 tablespoon butter. Cube remaining butter and set aside. Line two 15-in. x 10-in. x 1-in. pans with foil; brush with melted butter. Arrange jelly beans evenly in pans.

2. In a large saucepan, combine the sugar, corn syrup and water. Bring to a boil over medium heat, stirring constantly, until a candy thermometer reads 240° (soft-ball stage). Stir in cubed butter and salt. Cook and stir until mixture reaches 300° (hard-crack stage). Remove from the heat. Stir in baking soda (mixture will foam). Immediately pour over jelly beans. Spread with a buttered metal spatula. Cool; break into pieces. **Yield:** 2-1/2 pounds.

    Editor's Note: We recommend that you test your candy thermometer before each use by bringing water to a boil; the thermometer should read 212°. Adjust your recipe temperature up or down based on your test.

Marshmallow Easter Eggs *–Betty Claycomb, Alverton, Pennsylvania*

  25 **cups all-purpose flour (about 8 pounds)**
   1 **large egg**
   2 **tablespoons unflavored gelatin**
1/2 **cup cold water**
   2 **cups sugar**
   1 **cup light corn syrup, *divided***
3/4 **cup hot water**
   2 **teaspoons vanilla extract**
   1 **pound dark chocolate candy coating, melted**
   2 **ounces white candy coating, melted**

1. Spread 7 cups flour in each of three 13-in. x 9-in. x 2-in. pans and 4 cups flour in a 9-in. square pan. Carefully wash the egg in a mild bleach solution (1 teaspoon chlorine bleach to 1 qt. warm water); dry. Press washed egg halfway into the flour to form an impression. Repeat 35 times; set aside.

2. In a small bowl, sprinkle gelatin over cold water; set aside. In a large saucepan, combine sugar, 1/2 cup corn syrup and hot water. Bring to a boil over medium heat, stirring constantly, until a candy thermometer reads 238° (soft-ball stage). Remove from heat; stir in remaining corn syrup.

3. Pour into a large mixing bowl. Add reserved gelatin, 1 tablespoon at a time, beating on high until candy is thick and has cooled to lukewarm, about 10 minutes. Beat in vanilla. Spoon gelatin mixture into egg depressions; dust with flour. Let stand for 3-4 hours or until set.

4. Brush excess flour off marshmallow eggs. Dip each in chocolate candy coating. Place flat side down on waxed paper. Let stand until set. Pour white candy coating into a heavy-duty resealable plastic bag; cut a hole in one corner. Drizzle over eggs. **Yield:** 3 dozen.

    Editor's Note: For safety reasons, we recommend that you discard the egg and all of the flour. We recommend that you test your candy thermometer before each use by bringing water to a boil; the thermometer should read 212°. Adjust your recipe temperature up or down based on your test.

White Chocolate Easter Eggs *–Diane Hixon, Niceville, Florida*

1/2 **cup butter**
   3 **cups confectioners' sugar**
2/3 **cup sweetened condensed milk**
   1 **teaspoon vanilla extract**
   2 **cups finely chopped pecans**
   1 **pound white candy coating, melted**
Gel food coloring, optional

1. In a large saucepan, melt butter. Stir in confectioners' sugar, milk and vanilla until smooth. Stir in pecans. Transfer to a bowl. Cover and refrigerate 2 hours or until easy to handle. Drop by level tablespoonfuls onto waxed paper-lined baking sheets. Form into egg shapes. Cover and refrigerate overnight.

2. Dip eggs into candy coating. Place on waxed paper until set. If a speckled look is desired, dip a small crumpled ball of waxed paper into food coloring. First gently press waxed paper onto a paper plate to remove excess food coloring, then gently press color onto eggs. Repeat if needed. Blot eggs with a paper towel. **Yield:** about 4 dozen.

Braided Egg Bread —Marlene Jeffery, Holland, Manitoba

3-1/4 to 3-3/4 cups all-purpose flour
1 tablespoon sugar
1 package (1/4 ounce) active dry yeast
3/4 teaspoon salt
3/4 cup water
3 tablespoons vegetable oil
2 eggs
TOPPING:
1 egg
1 teaspoon water
1/2 teaspoon poppy seeds

1. In a mixing bowl, combine 1-1/2 cups flour, sugar, yeast and salt. In a saucepan, heat water and oil to 120°-130°. Add to dry ingredients with eggs and blend well. Beat on medium speed for 3 minutes. Stir in enough remaining flour to form a soft dough.

2. Turn onto a floured surface; knead until smooth and elastic, about 6-8 minutes. Place in a greased bowl, turning once to grease top. Cover and let rise in a warm place until doubled, about 1-1/2 hours.

3. Punch dough down. Turn onto a lightly floured surface. Set a third of the dough aside. Divide remaining dough into three pieces. Shape

each portion into a 13-in. rope. Place ropes on a greased baking sheet and braid; pinch ends to seal and tuck under. Divide reserved dough into three equal pieces; shape each into a 14-in. rope. Braid ropes. Center 14-in. braid on top of the shorter braid. Pinch ends to seal and tuck under. Cover and let rise until doubled, about 30 minutes.

4. Beat egg and water; brush over dough. Sprinkle with poppy seeds. Bake at 375° for 25-30 minutes or until golden brown. Cover with foil during the last 15 minutes of baking. Remove from pan to a wire rack to cool. **Yield:** 1 loaf.

Easter Nest Coffee Cake —Diane Burge, Friedheim, Missouri

3-3/4 to 4-1/4 cups all-purpose flour
1/4 cup sugar
1 package (1/4 ounce) active dry yeast
1 teaspoon salt
1/2 cup milk
1/4 cup water
1/4 cup butter
1 egg
GLAZE:
1 cup confectioners' sugar
1/4 teaspoon vanilla extract
2 to 3 tablespoons milk
Assorted colored sugar
1/2 teaspoon water
3 drops green food coloring
1 cup flaked coconut

1. In a large mixing bowl, combine 2 cups of flour, sugar, yeast and salt. In a saucepan, heat the milk, water and butter to 120°-130°. Add to dry ingredients; beat until blended. Add egg and 1/2 cup flour; beat until smooth. Stir in enough remaining flour to form a soft dough.

2. Turn onto a lightly floured surface; knead until smooth and elastic, about 4-6 minutes. Place in a greased bowl, turning once to grease top. Cover and let rise in a warm place until doubled, about 1 hour.

3. Punch dough down. Turn onto a lightly floured surface; divide into thirds. Cover and let rest for 10 minutes. Shape one portion of dough into six egg-shaped rolls. Arrange rolls with sides touching in the center of a large greased baking sheet. Roll each remaining portion of dough into 24-in. ropes; twist together. Wrap around the rolls; pinch ends together to seal.

4. Cover and let rise until doubled, about 45 minutes. Bake at 375° for 15-20 minutes or until golden brown. Remove from pan to a wire rack to cool.

5. For glaze, combine the confectioners' sugar, vanilla and enough milk to achieve drizzling consistency. Drizzle over coffee cake. Immediately sprinkle eggs with colored sugar. For grass, combine water and food coloring in a jar with a tight-fitting lid. Add coconut; shake until tinted. Sprinkle around edge of coffee cake nest. **Yield:** 1 loaf.

Poppy Seed Easter Cake
—Gena Aschleman, West Columbia, South Carolina

1-1/4 cups butter, softened
1-1/2 cups sugar
    4 eggs
    2 cups (16 ounces) sour cream
1/4 cup milk
    2 tablespoons lemon juice
    1 to 2 tablespoons grated lemon peel
    1 teaspoon vanilla extract
    3 cups all-purpose flour
    2 teaspoons baking powder
    2 teaspoons baking soda
1/4 teaspoon salt
1/4 cup poppy seeds
FROSTING:
    2 packages (8 ounces *each*) cream
        cheese, softened
    1 cup butter, softened
    8 cups confectioners' sugar
    2 to 3 tablespoons milk
Green food coloring
1/2 cup jelly beans

1. In a large mixing bowl, cream butter and sugar. Add eggs, one at a time, beating well after each addition. Combine the sour cream, milk, lemon juice, peel and vanilla; add to creamed mixture.

Combine the flour, baking powder, baking soda and salt; add to the creamed mixture and beat just until combined. Stir in poppy seeds (batter will be thick).

2. Transfer to three greased and floured 9-in. round baking pans. Bake at 350° for 25-30 minutes or until a toothpick inserted near the center comes out clean. Cool for 10 minutes before removing from pans to wire racks.

3. For frosting, in a mixing bowl, beat cream cheese and butter until light and fluffy. Gradually beat in sugar. Beat in enough milk to achieve spreading consistency. Place 1 cup of frosting in a small bowl and tint pale green; set aside.

4. To assemble, place one cake layer on a serving plate; frost top with white frosting. Repeat. Top with remaining cake layer. Frost top and sides of cake with remaining frosting.

5. Cut a small hole in the corner of a pastry or plastic bag; insert round tip No. 3. Fill bag with green frosting. Write "Happy Easter" on top of cake. With multi-opening or grass tip No. 233, pipe green frosting on top of cake to resemble a bird's nest. Pipe green frosting around top edge of cake. Place jelly beans in nest. Store in the refrigerator. **Yield:** 14-16 servings.

Editor's Note: A coupler and round tip No. 2 may be used in place of multi-opening tip No. 233.

Spinach Crescents —*Susan James, Manhattan, Kansas*

1/2 **cup sliced almonds**
1 **package (10 ounces) frozen chopped spinach, thawed and squeezed dry**
1/2 **cup grated Parmesan cheese**
1/4 **cup chopped onion**
2 **teaspoons olive oil**
1/4 **teaspoon salt**
1/8 **teaspoon pepper**
1 **package (8 ounces) refrigerated crescent rolls**

1. In a food processor or blender, finely chop the almonds. Add spinach, Parmesan cheese, onion, oil, salt and pepper; cover and process until well blended.

2. Unroll and separate the crescent dough into eight pieces. Spread spinach mixture evenly over dough to within 1/8 in. of edges. Roll up and place on a greased baking sheet. Bake at 375° for 15-18 minutes or until golden brown. Serve warm. **Yield:** 8 servings.

Lemon Clouds with Custard —*Jessica Wallace, Fort Worth, Texas*

11 **tablespoons sugar,** *divided*
3 **tablespoons cornstarch**
2 **teaspoons grated lemon peel**
1-1/3 **cups plus 1 tablespoon cold water,** *divided*
1/3 **cup lemon juice**
3 **egg whites**
1/8 **teaspoon cream of tartar**
CUSTARD SAUCE:
3 **tablespoons sugar**
1 **tablespoon cornstarch**
1-3/4 **cups cold milk**
3 **egg yolks, lightly beaten**
1/2 **teaspoon vanilla extract**

1. In a heavy saucepan, combine 5 tablespoons sugar, cornstarch and lemon peel. Gradually stir in 1-1/3 cups water until blended. Bring to a boil; cook and stir for 1-2 minutes or until thickened. Remove from the heat; stir in lemon juice. Set aside.

2. In another heavy saucepan, combine the egg whites, cream of tartar and remaining sugar and water. With a portable mixer, beat on low speed over low heat for 1 minute. Continue beating until mixture reaches 160°. Pour into a large mixing bowl. Beat on high speed until stiff peaks form. Fold into lemon syrup. Cover and refrigerate for at least 2 hours.

3. For sauce, in a small saucepan, combine sugar and cornstarch. Gradually stir in milk until smooth. Cook and stir over medium-high until thickened and bubbly. Reduce heat; cook and stir for 2 minutes longer. Remove from the heat. Stir a small amount of hot milk mixture into egg yolks; return all to pan, stirring constantly. Bring to a gentle boil; cook and stir 2 minutes longer. Remove from the heat. Gently stir in vanilla. Cover and refrigerate until chilled. Spoon lemon meringue into dessert cups; top with custard sauce. **Yield:** 5-6 servings.

Editor's Note: A stand mixer is recommended for beating the egg whites after they reach 160°.

Halloween

Candy Corn Cupcakes —Renee Schwebach, Dumont, Minnesota

1/2 cup shortening
1-1/2 cups sugar
1 teaspoon vanilla extract
2 cups all-purpose flour
3-1/2 teaspoons baking powder
1 teaspoon salt
1 cup milk
4 egg whites
Frosting of your choice
Candy corn *or* other decorations

1. In a mixing bowl, cream shortening and sugar. Beat in vanilla. Combine flour, baking powder and salt; add to the creamed mixture alternately with milk. Beat in the egg whites. Fill greased or paper-lined muffin cups half full.

2. Bake at 350° for 18-22 minutes or until a toothpick comes out clean. Cool for 10 minutes before removing from pans to wire racks. Frost cooled cupcakes; decorate as desired. **Yield:** 2 dozen.

Cookie Sticks —*Kathy Zielicke, Fond du Lac, Wisconsin*

1/2 cup vegetable oil
1/2 cup sugar
1/2 cup packed brown sugar
1 egg
1 teaspoon vanilla extract
1-1/2 cups all-purpose flour
1/2 teaspoon baking soda
1/2 teaspoon salt
1 cup (6 ounces) semisweet chocolate chips
1/2 cup chopped walnuts, optional

1. In a mixing bowl, combine the oil, sugars, egg and vanilla; mix well. Combine flour, baking soda and salt; gradually add to sugar mixture. Divide dough in half.

2. On a greased baking sheet, shape each portion into a 15-in. x 3-in. rectangle about 3 in. apart. Sprinkle chocolate chips and nuts if desired over dough; press lightly. Bake at 375° for 6-7 minutes. (Bake for 8-9 minutes for crispier cookies.) Cool for 5 minutes. Cut with a serrated knife into 1-in. strips; remove to wire racks to cool. **Yield:** about 3 dozen.

Peanut Butter Candy Pie —*Laura Mahaffey, Annapolis, Maryland*

1/4 cup butter
4 cups miniature marshmallows
6 cups crisp rice cereal
50 milk chocolate kisses *or*
    1-1/3 cups milk chocolate chips
1/2 cup flaked coconut
2 cups Reese's Pieces

1. In a microwave-safe bowl, heat the butter and marshmallows on high for 1 minute; stir until marshmallows are melted. Add the cereal; mix well. Press onto the bottom and up the sides of two greased 9-in. pie plates.

2. In a microwave or heavy saucepan, melt chocolate kisses; stir until smooth. Spread over prepared crusts. Sprinkle with coconut and candy pieces; press down lightly. Let stand until chocolate is set. Cut into slices. **Yield:** 2 pies (8 slices each).

Editor's Note: This recipe was tested in an 850-watt microwave.

Quick Ghost Cookies —*Denise Smith, Lusk, Wyoming*

1 **pound white candy coating, cut into chunks**
1 **package (1 pound) Nutter Butter peanut butter cookies**
Mini semisweet chocolate chips

1. In top of double boiler over simmering water, melt candy coating, stirring occasionally. Dip cookies into coating, covering completely. Set on waxed paper to cool.

2. Brush ends with a pastry brush dipped in coating where fingers touched cookies. While coating is still warm, place two chips on each cookie for eyes. **Yield:** about 3 dozen.

Halloween Peanut Bars —*Peg Woitel, Fairbanks, Alaska*

2 **cups quick-cooking oats**
1-1/2 **cups all-purpose flour**
3/4 **cup packed brown sugar**
1-1/2 **teaspoons baking soda**
1/2 **teaspoon salt**
3/4 **cup butter, melted**
1 **package (14 ounces) peanut M&M's**
1 **can (14 ounces) sweetened condensed milk**
1/2 **cup chunky peanut butter**
1 **tablespoon vanilla extract**

1. In a mixing bowl, combine the oats, flour, brown sugar, baking soda and salt. Add butter; mix until crumbly. Set aside 1 cup. Press the remaining crumb mixture into a greased 13-in. x 9-in. x 2-in. baking pan. Bake at 350° for 9-11 minutes or until edges are lightly browned (bars will puff up slightly).

2. Meanwhile, set aside 1 cup M&M's; chop remaining M&M's. In a mixing bowl, combine the milk, peanut butter and vanilla; mix well. Stir in chopped M&M's. Pour over crust; carefully spread evenly. Sprinkle with reserved M&M's; gently press into peanut butter mixture. Sprinkle with reserved crumb mixture. Bake 18-22 minutes longer or until edges are lightly browned. Cool on a wire rack before cutting. **Yield:** 3 dozen.

Black Widow Bites —*Taste of Home Test Kitchen*

Black shoestring licorice
    12 grape Jujubes
     1 cup vanilla *or* white chips
    24 red nonpareils
    12 chocolate wafers

1. Cut licorice into 96 pieces, about 1/2 in. long. Cut each piece lengthwise in half or quarters if necessary for thinner pieces. Using a toothpick, poke one licorice piece about 1/8 in. into a candy. Repeat seven times to make eight spider legs. Repeat with remaining licorice pieces and candy.

2. Melt chips in a microwave or heavy saucepan; stir until smooth. Transfer to a heavy-duty resealable plastic bag; cut a small hole in a corner of bag. Pipe two small dots on one candy and immediately place one nonpareil on each dot to create eyes. Repeat with remaining candies.

3. Pipe a web on each chocolate wafer. Pipe a dot of melted vanilla chips onto the bottom of the spider and attach to wafer. **Yield:** 1 dozen.

Pumpkin Whoopie Pies —*Deb Stuber, Carlisle, Pennsylvania*

    1 cup shortening
    2 cups packed brown sugar
    2 eggs
    1 teaspoon vanilla extract
3-1/2 cups all-purpose flour
1-1/2 teaspoons baking powder
1-1/2 teaspoons baking soda
    1 teaspoon salt
    1 teaspoon ground cinnamon
    1 teaspoon ground ginger
1-1/2 cups canned pumpkin
FILLING:
    1/4 cup all-purpose flour
Dash salt
    3/4 cup milk
    1 cup shortening
    2 cups confectioners' sugar
    2 teaspoons vanilla extract

1. In a mixing bowl, cream the shortening and brown sugar. Add eggs, one at a time, beating well after each addition. Beat in vanilla. Combine the flour, baking powder, baking soda, salt, cinnamon and ginger; add to creamed mixture alternately with pumpkin.

2. Drop by rounded tablespoonfuls 2 in. apart onto greased baking sheets; flatten slightly with the back of a spoon. Bake at 400° for 10-11 minutes. Remove to wire racks to cool.

3. For filling, combine the flour and salt in a saucepan. Gradually whisk in milk until smooth; cook and stir over medium heat for 5-7 minutes or until thickened. Cover and refrigerate until completely cooled.

4. In a mixing bowl, cream shortening, confectioners' sugar and vanilla. Add chilled milk mixture; beat for 7 minutes or until fluffy. Spread on the bottom of half of the cookies; top with remaining cookies. Store in the refrigerator. **Yield:** about 2 dozen.

Halloween Layer Cake —*Karen Wirth, Tavistock, Ontario*

  1 cup butter, softened
  2 cups sugar
  4 eggs
  3 cups all-purpose flour
  1 tablespoon baking powder
1/2 teaspoon salt
  1 cup milk
1/4 cup baking cocoa
1/4 cup water
1/2 teaspoon vanilla extract
1/2 teaspoon orange extract
  1 tablespoon grated orange peel
 10 drops yellow food coloring
  6 drops red food coloring
FROSTING:
  3 packages (3 ounces *each*) cream
    cheese, softened
5-3/4 cups confectioners' sugar
  2 tablespoons milk
  8 drops yellow food coloring
  6 drops red food coloring
GLAZE:
  3 squares (1 ounce *each*) semisweet
    chocolate
1/3 cup heavy whipping cream
Candy corn

1. In a mixing bowl, cream butter and sugar until light and fluffy. Add eggs, one at a time, beating well after each. Combine flour, baking powder and salt; add alternately with milk to creamed mixture. Mix well.

2. In another bowl, combine cocoa, water and vanilla; stir in 2 cups cake batter. Pour into a greased and floured 9-in. round baking pan. To remaining batter, add orange extract, peel and food coloring to. Pour into two greased and floured 9-in. baking pans. Bake at 350° for 30 minutes or until toothpick inserted near center comes out clean.

3. In a mixing bowl, beat all frosting ingredients until smooth. Place one orange cake layer on a cake plate; spread with 1/2 cup frosting. Top with chocolate layer; spread with 1/2 cup frosting. Top with second orange layer. Frost the sides and top of cake.

4. Microwave the chocolate and cream on high 1-1/2 minutes or until melted, stirring once. Stir until smooth; let cool 2 minutes. Slowly pour over cake, letting glaze drizzle down sides. Garnish with candy corn. **Yield:** 12-16 servings.

Spiderweb Pumpkin Cheesecake —*Bev Kotowich, Winnipeg, Manitoba*

1-3/4 cups chocolate wafer crumbs
(about 28 wafers)
1/4 cup butter, melted
FILLING:
3 packages (8 ounces *each*) cream
cheese, softened
3/4 cup sugar
1/2 cup packed brown sugar
3 eggs
1 can (15 ounces) solid-pack pumpkin
2 tablespoons cornstarch
3 teaspoons vanilla extract
1-1/2 teaspoons pumpkin pie spice
TOPPING:
2 cups (16 ounces) sour cream
3 tablespoons sugar
2 teaspoons vanilla extract
SPIDERWEB GARNISH:
1 cup sugar
1/8 teaspoon cream of tartar
1/3 cup water
4 squares (1 ounce *each*) semisweet
chocolate, melted

1. Combine wafer crumbs and butter; press onto the bottom and 1 in. up the sides of a greased 10-in. springform pan. Set aside. In a mixing bowl, beat cream cheese and sugars until smooth. Add eggs; beat on low speed just until combined. Whisk in pumpkin, cornstarch, vanilla and pumpkin pie spice just until blended. Pour into crust. Place pan on a baking sheet. Bake at 350° for 60-65 minutes or until center is almost set. Cool on a wire rack for 10 minutes.

2. Combine topping ingredients; spread over filling. Bake at 350° for 6 minutes. Cool on a wire rack for 10 minutes. Carefully run a knife around edge of pan to loosen; cool 1 hour longer. Refrigerate overnight. Remove sides of pan; set aside.

3. For spiderwebs, draw six 3-in. x 2-in. half circles on two sheets of parchment paper. Place another sheet of parchment paper on top; tape both securely to work surface. In a saucepan, bring the sugar, cream of tartar and water to a boil over medium heat. Boil, without stirring, until mixture turns a light amber color and a candy thermometer reads 350°. Immediately remove from the heat and stir. Cool, stirring occasionally, for 10-15 minutes or until hot sugar mixture falls off a metal spoon in a fine thread.

4. Using a spoon or meat fork, carefully drizzle syrup over half-circle outlines and inside the outlines to form spiderwebs; reheat syrup if needed. Cool completely. Place melted chocolate in a resealable plastic bag; cut a small hole in a corner of bag. Pipe 1-in. spiders onto parchment or foil; cool completely. With remaining melted chocolate, pipe two or three dots on each web; attach spiders.

5. Remove sides of springform pan. Cut cheesecake; place a web on top of each slice and remaining spiders on the side. Refrigerate leftovers. **Yield:** 12 servings.

Editor's Note: We recommend that you test your candy thermometer before each use by bringing water to a boil; the thermometer should read 212°. Adjust your recipe temperature up or down based on your test. Webs and spiders can be made in advance and stored at room temperature in an airtight container.

Cream Puff Monsters –*Susan Seymour, Valatie, New York*

3/4 cup plus 2 tablespoons all-purpose
     flour
2 tablespoons sugar
2 tablespoons baking cocoa
1 cup water
1/2 cup butter
4 eggs
1 package (3.9 ounces) instant
     chocolate pudding mix
2 cups cold milk
Yellow, red, blue and green food coloring
1 can (16 ounces) vanilla frosting
Sprinkles, small candies and slivered almonds

1. Combine flour, sugar and cocoa; set aside. In a saucepan over medium heat, bring water and butter to a boil; reduce heat to low. Add flour mixture all at once; stir until a smooth ball forms. Remove from the heat; let stand 5 minutes. Add eggs, one at a time, beating well after each. Beat until smooth.

2. Cover baking sheets with foil; grease foil. Drop batter by tablespoonfuls at least 2 in. apart onto baking sheets. Bake at 400° for 25-30 minutes or until lightly browned. Lift foil and transfer to a wire rack. Immediately cut a slit in each puff to allow steam to escape; cool.

3. Beat pudding mix and milk according to package directions; chill. When puffs are cool, split and remove soft dough from inside. Spoon pudding into puffs; replace tops.

4. Following food coloring package directions, combine red and yellow to make orange, and red and blue to make purple. Divide frosting among three microwave-safe bowls; tint with orange, purple and green food coloring. Microwave frosting until thin (not runny).

5. Spoon one or more colors onto puffs. Add sprinkles and candy for eyes; use almonds for teeth or whiskers. Chill. **Yield:** 2 dozen.

Frosty Ginger Pumpkin Squares –*Kathryn Reeger, Shelocta, Pennsylvania*

1/4 cup butter, melted
1 cup crushed graham crackers
     (about 16 squares)
1 cup crushed gingersnaps (about 18
     cookies)
2 cups canned pumpkin
1 cup sugar
1/2 to 1 teaspoon ground cinnamon
1/2 teaspoon salt
1/2 teaspoon ground ginger
1/4 teaspoon ground nutmeg
1 cup chopped walnuts
2 quarts vanilla ice cream, softened
     slightly

1. In a bowl, combine the butter and crushed graham crackers and gingersnaps. Press half of the crumb mixture into an ungreased 13-in. x 9-in. x 2-in. dish.

2. In a bowl, combine the pumpkin, sugar, cinnamon, salt, ginger and nutmeg. Stir in walnuts. Fold in ice cream. Spoon over crust. Sprinkle with remaining crumb mixture. Freeze until firm, about 3 hours. **Yield:** 12-15 servings.

Witch Hat Treats –Nancy Foust, Stoneboro, Pennsylvania

3 tablespoons butter
1 package (10 ounces) large
   marshmallows
1/2 cup peanut butter
6 cups crisp rice cereal
1-1/2 cups milk chocolate chips
1 teaspoon shortening
Orange frosting
Chocolate jimmies
Black rope licorice

1. In a large microwave-safe bowl, melt butter on high for about 45 seconds. Add marshmallows; stir to coat. Microwave on high for 45 seconds; stir. Microwave 45 seconds longer or until smooth. Stir in peanut butter. Immediately add cereal; stir gently until coated. Press into a greased 13-in. x 9-in. x 2-in. pan.

2. In a small microwave-safe bowl, heat chocolate chips and shortening on 70% power for 1 minute. Heat in 10- to 20-second intervals until melted; stir until smooth. Spread over cereal mixture. Cool completely.

3. Cut into 2-1/2-in. x 2-in. triangles with a thin base on bottom of triangle for hat brim. Decorate with frosting, jimmies for the buckle and licorice for the brim. **Yield:** 2 dozen.

   Editor's Note: This recipe was tested in an 850-watt microwave.

Wiggly Pumpkins –Frances Poste, Wall, South Dakota

2 packages (6 ounces *each*) orange
   gelatin
2-1/2 cups boiling water
1 cup cold milk
1 package (3.4 ounces) instant vanilla
   pudding mix
Candy corn
Black licorice *and/or* gumdrops

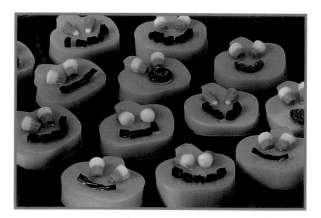

1. Dissolve gelatin in water; set aside for 30 minutes. Whisk milk and pudding mix until smooth, about 1 minute. Pour into gelatin; whisk until blended.

2. Pour into 13-in. x 9-in. x 2-in. pan coated with nonstick cooking spray. Chill until set. Cut into circles or use a pumpkin-shaped cookie cutter. Just before serving, add the candy eyes and mouths. **Yield:** 14-16 servings.

Thanksgiving

Spiced Pumpkin Pie —*Pat Marken, Hansville, Washington*

3 eggs
1 cup milk
1/2 cup sugar
1/2 cup packed brown sugar
1 teaspoon ground cinnamon
3/4 teaspoon ground nutmeg
1/2 teaspoon salt
1/2 teaspoon ground ginger
1/2 teaspoon ground cloves
1 can (15 ounces) solid-pack pumpkin
1 unbaked pastry shell (9 inches)
Whipped topping and additional
  ground cinnamon

1. In a bowl, lightly beat eggs. Add the milk, sugars, cinnamon, nutmeg, salt, ginger and cloves; mix well. Stir in the pumpkin just until blended.

2. Pour into pastry shell. Bake at 350° for 50-60 minutes or until a knife inserted near the center comes out clean. Cool on a wire rack. Chill until serving. Garnish with whipped topping sprinkled with cinnamon. Refrigerate leftovers. **Yield:** 6-8 servings.

Pumpkin Pecan Loaves —*Brenda Jackson, Garden City, Kansas*

3-1/3 cups all-purpose flour
   3 cups sugar
   2 teaspoons baking soda
1-1/2 teaspoons salt
   1 teaspoon ground cinnamon
   1 teaspoon ground nutmeg
   1 can (15 ounces) solid-pack pumpkin
   1 cup vegetable oil
   4 eggs, lightly beaten
 2/3 cup water
 1/2 cup chopped pecans
CARAMEL GLAZE:
 1/4 cup butter
 1/4 cup sugar
 1/4 cup packed brown sugar
 1/4 cup heavy whipping cream
 2/3 cup confectioners' sugar
   1 teaspoon vanilla extract

1. In a bowl, combine the first six ingredients. Combine the pumpkin, oil, eggs and water. Stir into dry ingredients just until combined; fold in the pecans.

2. Spoon into two greased 9-in. x 5-in. x 3-in. loaf pans. Bake at 350° for 60-65 minutes or until a toothpick inserted near the center comes out clean. Cool for 10 minutes before removing from pans to wire racks.

3. For glaze, combine the butter, sugars and cream in a saucepan. Cook until sugar is dissolved. Cool for 20 minutes. Stir in the confectioners' sugar and vanilla until smooth. Drizzle over cooled loaves. **Yield:** 2 loaves.

Sweet Potato Crescents —*Rebecca Bailey, Fairbury, Nebraska*

   2 packages (1/4 ounce *each*) active dry yeast
   1 cup warm water (110° to 115°)
   1 can (15 ounces) cut sweet potatoes, drained and mashed
 1/2 cup sugar
 1/2 cup shortening
   1 egg
1-1/2 teaspoons salt
   5 to 5-1/2 cups all-purpose flour
 1/4 cup butter, melted

1. In a large mixing bowl, dissolve yeast in water; let stand for 5 minutes. Beat in the sweet potatoes, sugar, shortening, egg, salt and 3 cups flour. Stir in enough remaining flour to form a stiff dough.

2. Turn onto a floured surface; knead until smooth and elastic, about 6-8 minutes. Place in a greased bowl, turning once to grease top. Cover and let rise in a warm place until doubled, about 1 hour.

3. Punch dough down; divide into thirds. Roll each portion into a 12-in. circle; cut each into 12 wedges. Brush with butter. Roll up from the wide end and place point side down, 2 in. apart on greased baking sheets. Cover and let rise until doubled, about 40 minutes.

4. Bake at 375° for 13-15 minutes or until golden brown. Remove from pans to wire racks. **Yield:** 3 dozen.

Saucy Spiced Apple Pie —Lisa Jedrzejczak, Copac, Michigan

Pastry for double-crust pie (9 inches)
- 1/4 cup butter, softened
- 2 cups sugar
- 1 egg
- 1 egg, *separated*
- 1/3 cup unsweetened pineapple juice
- 1-1/2 teaspoons vanilla extract
- 1/3 cup all-purpose flour
- 1/2 teaspoon ground cinnamon
- 1/4 teaspoon ground ginger
- 1/4 teaspoon ground nutmeg
- 6 cups sliced peeled tart apples

Additional sugar

1. Line a 9-in. pie plate with bottom pastry; trim even with edge. In a mixing bowl, cream butter and sugar. Add egg, egg yolk, pineapple juice and vanilla; mix well (mixture will appear curdled).

2. Combine the flour, cinnamon, ginger and nutmeg; add to creamed mixture. Fill the crust with apple slices. Top with the creamed mixture.

3. Roll out remaining pastry to fit top of pie; place over filling. Trim, seal and flute edges. Cut slits in top. Beat egg white; brush over pastry. Sprinkle with additional sugar. Bake at 350° for 55-60 minutes or until crust is golden brown and filling is bubbly. Cool on a wire rack. Refrigerate leftovers. **Yield:** 6-8 servings.

Maple Squash Soup —Pat Hoffman, Pensacola, Florida

- 4 medium butternut squash (about 2-1/4 pounds *each*)
- 4 teaspoons plus 1/2 cup butter, *divided*
- 1/2 teaspoon salt
- 1/4 teaspoon pepper
- 3 cups chopped onions
- 1 medium leek, chopped
- 1 celery rib, chopped
- 3 cans (14-1/2 ounces *each*) vegetable *or* chicken broth
- 1 cup maple syrup

Additional maple syrup
- 1/4 teaspoon ground nutmeg

1. Pierce neck end of squash in several places with a sharp knife. Microwave, uncovered, on high for 4-5 minutes. Cut squash between neck and bulb. Peel neck and cut into cubes; set aside. Remove and discard seeds and membrane from bulb, leaving about a 1/2-in. shell. Place 1 teaspoon of butter in each shell; sprinkle with salt and pepper.

2. Place in a foil-lined 13-in. x 9-in. x 2-in. baking pan. Bake at 350° for 15-20 minutes or until butter is melted and squash is heated through.

3. In a soup kettle, saute onions, leek and celery in remaining butter until tender. Add squash cubes, broth and syrup; bring to a boil. Reduce heat; cover and simmer for 20 minutes or until squash is tender.

4. In a blender, puree soup in small batches until smooth. Return to the pan. Drizzle additional syrup into squash bowls. Fill with soup; drizzle with syrup if desired. Sprinkle with nutmeg. Freeze remaining soup. **Yield:** 3 quarts (4 soup bowls).

Cranberry Sweet Potato Muffins —Diane Musil, Lyons, Illinois

1-1/2 cups all-purpose flour
  1/2 cup sugar
    2 teaspoons baking powder
  3/4 teaspoon salt
  1/2 teaspoon ground cinnamon
  1/2 teaspoon ground nutmeg
    1 egg
  1/2 cup milk
  1/2 cup cold mashed sweet potatoes
      (without added butter or milk)
  1/4 cup butter, melted
    1 cup chopped fresh *or* frozen
      cranberries
Cinnamon-sugar

1. In a bowl, combine flour, sugar, baking powder, salt, cinnamon and nutmeg. In a small bowl, combine egg, milk, sweet potatoes and butter; stir into dry ingredients just until moistened. Stir in cranberries.

2. Fill greased or paper-lined muffin cups half full. Sprinkle with cinnamon-sugar. Bake at 375° for 18-22 minutes or until a toothpick inserted near center of muffin comes out clean. Cool in pan 10 minutes before removing to a wire rack. **Yield:** 1 dozen.

Festive Pumpkin Dip —Evelyn Kennell, Roanoke, Illinois

   12 ounces cream cheese, softened
  3/4 cup canned pumpkin
    2 tablespoons taco seasoning mix
  1/8 teaspoon garlic powder
  1/3 cup chopped dried beef
  1/3 cup chopped green pepper
  1/3 cup chopped sweet red pepper
    1 can (2-1/4 ounces) sliced ripe olives,
      drained
    1 round loaf (1 pound) Italian *or*
      pumpernickel bread
Fresh vegetables, crackers *or* corn chips

1. In a mixing bowl, beat cream cheese, pumpkin, taco seasoning and garlic powder until smooth. Stir in beef, peppers and olives. Cover and refrigerate until serving.

2. Just before serving, cut top off bread; scoop out bread from inside, leaving a 1/2-in. shell

(save the bread from inside to make croutons or bread crumbs or save for another use). Fill shell with cream cheese mixture. Serve with vegetables, crackers or corn chips. **Yield:** 3 cups.

Apple Cheddar Scones —*Jeanne Alexander, Qnalicum Beach, British Columbia*

        1-3/4 **cups all-purpose flour**
            2 **tablespoons sugar**
        1-1/2 **teaspoons baking powder**
          1/2 **teaspoon salt**
          1/4 **teaspoon baking soda**
          1/3 **cup cold butter**
            1 **cup buttermilk**
            1 **cup (4 ounces) shredded cheddar
               cheese**
            1 **cup diced peeled apples**

1. In a bowl, combine the first five ingredients. Cut in butter until mixture resembles coarse crumbs. Stir in buttermilk just until moistened. Gently fold in the cheese and apples. Turn onto a floured surface; knead 10 times.

2. Pat into a 9-in. circle. Cut into eight wedges. Separate wedges and place on a greased baking sheet. Bake at 450° for 12-15 minutes or until golden brown. **Yield:** 8 scones.

Buttercup Squash Coffee Cake —*Mary Jones, Cumberland, Maine*

STREUSEL:
          1/4 **cup packed brown sugar**
          1/4 **cup sugar**
          1/4 **cup all-purpose flour**
          1/4 **cup quick-cooking oats**
          1/4 **cup chopped nuts**
        1-1/2 **teaspoons ground cinnamon**
            3 **tablespoons cold butter**
CAKE:
          1/2 **cup butter-flavored shortening**
            1 **cup sugar**
            2 **eggs**
            1 **cup mashed cooked buttercup squash**
            1 **teaspoon vanilla extract**
            2 **cups all-purpose flour**
            2 **teaspoons baking powder**
        1-1/2 **teaspoons ground cinnamon**
          1/2 **teaspoon baking soda**
          1/2 **teaspoon salt**
          1/4 **teaspoon ground ginger**
          1/4 **teaspoon ground nutmeg**
Pinch ground cloves
          1/2 **cup unsweetened applesauce**
GLAZE:
          1/2 **cup confectioners' sugar**
          1/4 **teaspoon vanilla extract**
        1-1/2 **teaspoons hot water**

1. Combine the first six ingredients. Cut in butter until crumbly; set aside. In a mixing bowl, cream shortening and sugar. Beat in the eggs, one at a time. Beat in squash and vanilla. Combine the dry ingredients; gradually add to creamed mixture.

2. Spoon half into a greased 9-in. springform pan. Spread applesauce over batter. Sprinkle with half of the streusel. Spoon remaining batter evenly over streusel. Top with remaining streusel. Bake at 350° for 50-55 minutes or until a toothpick inserted near center comes out clean. Cool for 10 minutes; remove sides of pan. Combine glaze ingredients; drizzle over coffee cake. **Yield:** 10-12 servings.

Bread Pudding Pumpkin –*Darlene Brenden, Salem, Oregon*

2 medium pie pumpkins (about 3 pounds *each*)
4 eggs, lightly beaten
1 can (14 ounces) sweetened condensed milk
1/2 cup packed brown sugar
1 teaspoon salt
1 teaspoon ground cinnamon
1 teaspoon vanilla extract
3/4 teaspoon ground nutmeg
6 cups cubed crustless day-old bread
1 can (8 ounces) crushed pineapple, drained
1 cup chopped walnuts
1 cup raisins

1. Wash pumpkins; cut off tops and discard. Scoop out seeds and loose fibers (save seeds for another use if desired).

2. In a large bowl, whisk the eggs, milk, brown sugar, salt, cinnamon, vanilla and nutmeg. Stir in bread cubes, pineapple, walnuts and raisins. Spoon into pumpkin shells.

3. Place on a greased 15-in. x 10-in. x 1-in. baking pan. Loosely cover tops with foil. Bake at 350° for 1-1/4 hours. Uncover; bake 15-30 minutes longer or until pumpkin is soft and a knife inserted near the center of bread pudding comes out clean. To serve, scoop bread pudding and cooked pumpkin into dessert dishes. **Yield:** 6-8 servings.

Cranberry Bundt Cake –*Lucile Cline, Wichita, Kansas*

3/4 cup butter, softened
1-1/2 cups sugar
3 eggs
1-1/2 teaspoons almond extract
3 cups all-purpose flour
1-1/2 teaspoons baking powder
1-1/2 teaspoons baking soda
1/2 teaspoon salt
1-1/2 cups (12 ounces) sour cream
1 can (16 ounces) whole-berry cranberry sauce
1/2 cup finely chopped pecans
ICING:
3/4 cup confectioners' sugar
4-1/2 teaspoons water
1/2 teaspoon almond extract

1. In a large mixing bowl, cream butter and sugar. Add eggs, one at a time, beating well after each addition. Stir in the extract. Combine the flour, baking powder, baking soda and salt; add to the creamed mixture alternately with sour cream, beating well after each addition. Spoon a third of the batter into a greased and floured 10-in. fluted tube pan. Top with a third of the cranberry sauce. Repeat layers twice. Sprinkle with pecans.

2. Bake at 350° for 65-70 minutes or until a toothpick inserted near the center comes out clean. Cool for 10 minutes before removing from pan to a wire rack. Combine icing ingredients until smooth; drizzle over warm cake. **Yield:** 12-16 servings.

Rustic Pear Tart –*Taste of Home Test Kitchen*

1-1/3 cups all-purpose flour
    3 tablespoons sugar
    1/4 teaspoon salt
    7 tablespoons cold butter, cubed
    2 to 3 tablespoons cold water
FILLING:
    3/4 cup sugar
    1/4 cup slivered almonds, toasted
    1/4 cup all-purpose flour
1-1/2 teaspoons grated lemon peel
    1/2 to 3/4 teaspoon ground cinnamon
    4 medium ripe pears, peeled and sliced
    1 tablespoon butter
GLAZE (optional):
    1/4 cup confectioners' sugar
1-1/2 teaspoons milk
    1/4 teaspoon vanilla extract
    1/4 cup slivered almonds, toasted

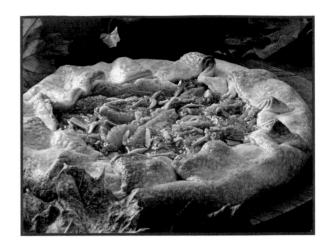

1. In a bowl, combine the flour, sugar and salt; cut in butter until crumbly. Gradually add water, tossing with a fork until dough forms a ball. Roll out to a 14-in. circle. Transfer pastry to a 14-in. pizza pan.

2. In a bowl, combine the sugar, almonds, flour, lemon peel and cinnamon. Add pears; toss to coat. Spoon over the pastry to within 2 in. of edges; dot with butter. Fold edges of pastry over pears. Bake at 375° for 45-50 minutes or until golden brown.

3. For glaze, combine the confectioners' sugar, milk and vanilla. Pour over warm tart. Sprinkle with almonds. Cool on a wire rack. **Yield:** 8-10 servings.

Curried Pumpkin Soup –*Kimberly Knepper, Euless, Texas*

1/2 pound fresh mushrooms, sliced
1/2 cup chopped onion
    2 tablespoons butter
    2 tablespoons all-purpose flour
1/2 to 1 teaspoon curry powder
    3 cups vegetable broth
    1 can (15 ounces) solid-pack pumpkin
    1 can (12 ounces) evaporated milk
    1 tablespoon honey
1/2 teaspoon salt
1/4 teaspoon pepper
1/4 teaspoon ground nutmeg
Fresh *or* frozen chives, optional

1. In a large saucepan, saute the mushrooms and onion in butter until tender. Stir in the flour and curry powder until blended.

2. Gradually add the broth. Bring to a boil; cook and stir for 2 minutes or until thickened. Add the pumpkin, milk, honey, salt, pepper and nutmeg; heat through. Garnish with chives if desired. **Yield:** 7 servings.

Cranberry Cheesecake —*Joy Monn, Stockbridge, Georgia*

1-1/2 cups cinnamon graham cracker
   crumbs (about 24 squares)
 1/4 cup sugar
 1/3 cup butter, melted
FILLING:
  4 packages (8 ounces *each*) cream
   cheese, softened
  1 can (14 ounces) sweetened
   condensed milk
 1/4 cup lemon juice
  4 eggs
1-1/2 cups chopped fresh *or* frozen
   cranberries
  1 teaspoon grated orange peel
Sugared cranberries and orange peel strips,
 optional

1. In a bowl, combine cracker crumbs and sugar; stir in butter. Press onto the bottom of a greased 9-in. springform pan; set aside.

2. In a mixing bowl, beat cream cheese and milk until smooth. Beat in lemon juice until smooth. Add eggs; beat on low speed just until combined. Fold in cranberries and orange peel.

Pour over the crust. Place pan on a baking sheet. Bake at 325° for 60-70 minutes or until center is almost set. Cool on a wire rack for 10 minutes.

3. Carefully run a knife around edge of pan to loosen. Cool 1 hour longer. Refrigerate for at least 6 hours or overnight. Remove sides of pan. Garnish with sugared cranberries and orange peel if desired. **Yield:** 12 servings.

Paradise Cran-Applesauce —*Sallie McQuay, Sayre, Pennsylvania*

  4 cups fresh *or* frozen cranberries
 1/4 cup water
  8 cups sliced peeled cooking apples
  2 cups sugar

1. In a covered saucepan, simmer cranberries and water for 20-25 minutes or until tender. Press through a sieve or food mill; return to the saucepan.

2. Add the apples; cover and simmer for 35-40 minutes or until apples are tender but retain their shape. Add sugar. Simmer for 5 minutes, stirring occasionally. **Yield:** 8-10 servings.

Cakes, Pies & Desserts

County Fair Cherry Pie —*Taste of Home Test Kitchen*

1-1/4 cups sugar
   2 tablespoons cornstarch
Dash salt
   4 cups pitted unsweetened sour cherries
Pastry for double-crust pie (9 inches)
Star cookie cutters (1/2 inch and 2 inches)
Confectioners' sugar

1. In a medium saucepan, combine sugar, cornstarch and salt; stir in cherries. Let stand for 30 minutes. Cook and stir over medium heat until mixture boils and starts to thicken. Pour into jars or freezer containers, leaving 1/2-in. headspace. Cool. Cover with lids; refrigerate or freeze.

2. To make pie, line a 9-in. pie plate with bottom pastry; add filling. (If filling is frozen, thaw in the refrigerator overnight.) Flute edges of pastry. Bake at 375° for 45 minutes or until crust is golden brown and filling is bubbly. Cover edges during the last 20 minutes to prevent overbrowning.

3. Meanwhile, cut remaining pastry into 12-14 large stars and 16-18 small stars; place on an ungreased baking sheet. Bake at 375° for 8-10 minutes or until golden brown. Remove to wire rack to cool. Sprinkle with confectioners' sugar. Place stars randomly over cooled pie. Sprinkle edges of pie with confectioners' sugar. **Yield:** 6-8 servings.

Orange Date Pound Cake —*Ruth Bartz, Suring, Wisconsin*

1 **cup butter, softened**
3 **cups sugar,** *divided*
4 **eggs**
1 **tablespoon orange peel,** *divided*
3 **cups all-purpose flour**
1 **teaspoon baking soda**
1-1/3 **cups buttermilk**
1 **pound chopped dates**
1 **cup coarsely chopped pecans**
1/2 **cup orange juice**

1. In a mixing bowl, cream butter and 2 cups sugar. Add the eggs, one at a time, beating well after each addition. Add 2 teaspoons orange peel. Combine flour and baking soda; add to the creamed mixture alternately with buttermilk. Stir in dates and pecans. Pour into a greased and floured 10-in. tube pan; spread evenly. Bake at 325° for 70-75 minutes or until a toothpick inserted near the center comes out clean.

2. Combine the orange juice and remaining sugar and orange peel; pour over cake. Cool for 30 minutes before removing from pan to a wire rack to cool completely. **Yield:** 12-16 servings.

Berry Big Pie —*Janelle Seward, Ontario, Oregon*

4 **cups all-purpose flour**
1 **tablespoon sugar**
2 **teaspoons salt**
1-3/4 **cups cold shortening**
1/2 **cup cold water**
1 **egg**
1 **tablespoon white vinegar**
FILLING:
8 **cups fresh** *or* **frozen blackberries**
2 **cups sugar**
1/2 **cup all-purpose flour**
Half-and-half cream

1. In a large bowl, combine flour, sugar and salt; cut in shortening until mixture resembles coarse crumbs. In a bowl, combine water, egg and vinegar; stir into flour mixture just until moistened. Form into a roll. Cover and refrigerate for 1 hour.

2. On a floured surface, roll two-thirds of the dough into an 18-in. x 14-in. rectangle. Carefully place onto the bottom and up the sides of a 13-in. x 9-in. x 2-in. glass baking dish. Combine berries, sugar and flour; pour into crust. Use the remaining dough to make lattice strips; place over the filling. Brush pastry with cream.

3. Bake at 400° for 15 minutes; reduce heat to 350°. Bake about 1 hour longer or until bubbly. Cool completely. Store in the refrigerator. **Yield:** 12-16 servings.

Editor's Note: If using frozen berries, do not thaw.

Tortilla Fruit Pie —*Taste of Home Test Kitchen*

  3 teaspoons butter, *divided*
  1 tablespoon brown sugar
  2 teaspoons lemon juice
1/8 teaspoon almond extract
  1 large ripe peach, peeled and sliced
  1 flour tortilla (10 inches)
  1 teaspoon sugar

1. In a small saucepan, melt 2 teaspoons butter. Stir in the brown sugar, lemon juice and extract. Add peach slices. Cook and stir over medium-low heat for 5 minutes.

2. Place tortilla on an ungreased baking sheet. Spoon peach mixture onto half of tortilla to within 1/2 in. of sides; fold tortilla over. Melt remaining butter; brush over the top. Sprinkle with sugar. Bake at 350° for 15-20 minutes or until golden brown. Cut in half. **Yield:** 1 serving.

Chocolate Mayonnaise Cake —*Deborah Amrine, Grand Haven, Michigan*

  2 cups all-purpose flour
  1 cup sugar
  3 tablespoons baking cocoa
  2 teaspoons baking soda
  1 cup water
  1 cup mayonnaise
  1 teaspoon vanilla extract
BROWN SUGAR FROSTING:
  1/4 cup butter
  1/2 cup packed brown sugar
  2 tablespoons milk
1-3/4 cups sifted confectioners' sugar

1. In a large mixing bowl, combine flour, sugar, cocoa and baking soda. Add water, mayonnaise and vanilla; beat on medium speed until thoroughly combined. Pour into a greased 9-in. square or 11-in. x 7-in. x 2-in. baking pan. Bake at 350° for 30-35 minutes or until a toothpick inserted near the center comes out clean. Cool completely.

2. For frosting, melt butter in a saucepan. Stir in brown sugar; cook and stir until bubbly. Remove from the heat and stir in milk. Gradually add confectioners' sugar; beat by hand until frosting is of spreading consistency. Immediately frost cake. **Yield:** 9-12 servings.

Pastel Four-Layer Cake —Bryan Anderson, Granit Falls, Minnesota

1 package (18-1/4 ounces) chocolate
   cake mix
3 tablespoons all-purpose flour
Pinch salt
1-1/2 cups milk
3/4 cup butter, softened
3/4 cup shortening
1-1/2 cups sugar
Yellow, red and green liquid food coloring
1/4 teaspoon *each* lemon, peppermint,
   almond and vanilla extract
3 tablespoons baking cocoa

1. Prepare and bake chocolate cake according to the package directions, using two greased and floured 9-in. round baking pans. Cool in pans for 10 minutes; remove cakes to wire racks to cool completely.

2. In a saucepan, combine flour and salt. Gradually add milk; cook and stir over medium-high heat until thick, about 5-7 minutes. Remove from the heat; cover and refrigerate until completely cool. In a mixing bowl, beat butter, shortening and sugar until sugar dissolves. Add chilled milk mixture; beat for 7 minutes.

3. Divide frosting equally among four bowls, with 1-1/4 cups in each. To the first bowl, add 2-3 drops yellow food coloring and lemon extract; mix well. To second bowl, add 2-3 drops red food coloring and peppermint extract. To third bowl, add 2-3 drops green food coloring and almond extract. To the last bowl, add the cocoa and vanilla.

4. Split cake layers in half horizontally; spread each layer with a different frosting. Stack layers, using cocoa-frosted layer for the top. Do not frost sides of cake. **Yield:** 12 servings.

Applesauce Lattice Pie —Cherie Sweet, Evansville, Indiana

1-1/2 cups all-purpose flour
3 tablespoons sugar
1/4 teaspoon plus 1/8 teaspoon baking
   powder
1/4 teaspoon plus 1/8 teaspoon salt
6 tablespoons cold butter
4 to 6 tablespoons cold water
4-1/2 teaspoons milk
1-1/2 teaspoons cider vinegar
FILLING:
5 cups sliced peeled tart apples
1/4 cup raisins
3 tablespoons sugar
2 tablespoons all-purpose flour
4 teaspoons brown sugar
2 teaspoons ground cinnamon
1-1/2 cups unsweetened applesauce
2 teaspoons butter

1. In a bowl, combine the flour, sugar, baking powder and salt; cut in butter until mixture resembles coarse crumbs. Combine the water, milk and vinegar; gradually add to crumb mixture, tossing with a fork until dough forms a ball.

2. Coat a 9-in. pie plate with nonstick cooking spray. Set aside a third of the dough. On a lightly floured surface, roll out remaining dough to fit a pie plate. Transfer pastry to pie plate; trim even with edge of plate.

3. In a large bowl, combine apples and raisins. Combine the sugar, flour, brown sugar and cinnamon; add to apple mixture and toss to coat. Spoon 3 cups into the crust; cover with applesauce. Top with remaining apple mixture; dot with butter.

4. Roll out reserved pastry; make a lattice crust. Trim and flute edges. Bake at 375° for 40-45 minutes or until crust is golden brown and filling is bubbly Cool on wire rack. **Yield:** 8 servings.

Pastel Four-Layer Cake

Country Apple Cobbler *–Mavis Diment, Marcus, Iowa*

1-1/3 cups sugar, *divided*
  1/4 cup water
    2 tablespoons quick-cooking tapioca
  1/4 teaspoon ground cinnamon
    6 cups thinly sliced peeled tart apples
     (about 5 medium)
    1 cup all-purpose flour
    1 teaspoon baking powder
  1/4 teaspoon salt
  1/3 cup butter, melted
  1/4 cup milk
1-1/2 cups (6 ounces) shredded cheddar
    cheese
  1/2 cup chopped walnuts
Whipped topping, optional

1. In a large saucepan, combine 1 cup sugar, water, tapioca and cinnamon. Bring to a boil over medium heat, stirring occasionally. Remove from the heat; stir in the apples until coated. Pour into a greased 8-in. baking dish; set aside.

2. In a small bowl, combine the flour, baking powder, salt and remaining sugar. Stir in butter and milk just until moistened. Fold in cheese and walnuts. Sprinkle over apple mixture. Bake at 375° for 30-35 minutes or until filling is bubbly. Serve with whipped topping if desired. **Yield:** 6-8 servings.

Peanut Butter Pie *–Doris Doherty, Albany, Oregon*

CRUST:
1-1/4 cups chocolate cookie crumbs
    (20 cookies)
  1/4 cup sugar
  1/4 cup butter, melted
FILLING:
    1 package (8 ounces) cream cheese,
     softened
    1 cup creamy peanut butter
    1 cup sugar
    1 tablespoon butter, softened
    1 teaspoon vanilla extract
    1 cup heavy whipping cream, whipped
Grated chocolate *or* chocolate cookie
  crumbs, optional

1. Combine crust ingredients; press into a 9-in. pie plate. Bake at 375° for 10 minutes. Cool to room temperate.

2. In a mixing bowl, beat cream cheese, peanut butter, sugar, butter and vanilla until smooth. Fold in whipped cream. Gently spoon into crust. Garnish with chocolate or cookie crumbs if desired. Store in the refrigerator. **Yield:** 8-10 servings.

Eggless Chocolate Cake
–Peggy Weed, Cheshire, Connecticut

    1 tablespoon plus 1/2 cup baking cocoa,
      divided
    3 cups all-purpose flour
    2 cups sugar
    2 teaspoons baking soda
    1 teaspoon salt
1/4 teaspoon ground cinnamon
    2 cups cold brewed coffee
1/3 cup canola oil
    2 tablespoons white vinegar
    2 teaspoons vanilla extract
1/2 cup semisweet chocolate chips
1/2 teaspoon shortening

1. Coat a 10-in. fluted tube pan with nonstick cooking spray and dust with 1 tablespoon cocoa; set aside. In a large bowl, combine the flour, sugar, baking soda, salt, cinnamon and remaining cocoa. In another bowl, combine the coffee, oil, vinegar and vanilla. Stir into dry ingredients just until combined. Pour into prepared pan.

2. Bake at 350° for 40-50 minutes or until a toothpick inserted near the center comes out clean. Cool for 10 minutes before removing from pan to a wire rack to cool completely.

3. In a microwave or heavy saucepan, melt chocolate chips and shortening; stir until smooth. Drizzle over cake. **Yield:** 14 servings.

Zucchini Cake
–Marie Hoyer, Hodgenville, Kentucky

2-1/2 cups all-purpose flour
    2 cups sugar
1-1/2 teaspoons ground cinnamon
    1 teaspoon salt
1/2 teaspoon baking powder
1/2 teaspoon baking soda
    1 cup vegetable oil
    4 eggs
    2 cups shredded zucchini
1/2 cup chopped walnuts, optional
FROSTING:
    1 package (3 ounces) cream cheese,
      softened
1/4 cup butter, softened
    1 tablespoon milk
    1 teaspoon vanilla extract
    2 cups confectioners' sugar
Additional chopped walnuts, optional

1. In a mixing bowl, combine flour, sugar, cinnamon, salt, baking powder and baking soda. Combine oil and eggs; add to dry ingredients. Add zucchini; stir until thoroughly combined. Fold in walnuts if desired.

2. Pour into a greased 13-in. x 9-in. x 2-in. baking pan. Bake at 350° for 35-40 minutes or until a toothpick inserted near the center comes out clean. Cool.

3. For frosting, in a small mixing bowl, beat cream cheese, butter, milk and vanilla until smooth. Add confectioners' sugar and mix well. Frost cake. Sprinkle with nuts if desired. Store in the refrigerator. **Yield:** 20-24 servings.

Candy Apple Pie —*Cindy Kleweno, Burlington, Colorado*

6 cups thinly sliced peeled tart apples
2 tablespoons lime juice
3/4 cup sugar
1/4 cup all-purpose flour
1/2 teaspoon ground cinnamon *or* nutmeg
1/4 teaspoon salt
Pastry for double-crust pie (9 inches)
2 tablespoons butter
TOPPING:
1/4 cup butter
1/2 cup packed brown sugar
2 tablespoons heavy whipping cream
1/2 cup chopped pecans

1. In a large bowl, toss apples with lime juice. Combine dry ingredients; add to the apples and toss lightly.

2. Line a 9-in. pie plate with bottom crust and trim even with edge; fill with apple mixture. Dot with butter. Roll out remaining pastry to fit top of pie. Place over filling. Trim, seal and flute edges high; cut steam vents. Bake at 400° for 40-45 minutes or until golden brown and apples are tender.

3. Meanwhile, melt butter in a small saucepan. Stir in brown sugar and cream; bring to a boil, stirring constantly. Remove from the heat and stir in pecans. Pour over top crust. Bake 3-4 minutes longer or until bubbly. Serve warm. **Yield:** 8 servings.

Milk Chocolate Bundt Cake –*Sharan Williams, Spanish Fork, Utah*

  1 milk chocolate candy bar (7 ounces)
1/2 cup chocolate syrup
  1 cup butter, softened
1-1/2 cups sugar
  4 eggs
  1 teaspoon vanilla extract
2-3/4 cups all-purpose flour
1/2 teaspoon salt
1/2 teaspoon baking soda
  1 cup buttermilk
Confectioners' sugar, optional

1. In a saucepan, heat the candy bar and chocolate syrup over low heat until melted; set aside to cool.

2. In a mixing bowl, cream butter and sugar. Add eggs, one at a time, beating well after each addition. Stir in chocolate mixture and vanilla. Combine flour, salt and baking soda; add to creamed mixture alternately with buttermilk.

3. Pour into a greased and floured 10-in. fluted tube pan. Bake at 350° for 65-70 minutes or until a toothpick inserted near the center comes out clean. Cool in pan on a wire rack for 15 minutes. Remove from pan and cool completely. Dust with confectioners' sugar if desired. **Yield:** 12-14 servings.

Black Forest Pie –*Trudy Black, Dedham, Massachusetts*

3/4 cup sugar
1/3 cup baking cocoa
  2 tablespoons all-purpose flour
1/3 cup milk
1/4 cup butter
  2 eggs, lightly beaten
  1 can (21 ounces) cherry pie filling,
    divided
  1 unbaked pastry shell (9 inches)
Whipped topping, optional

1. In a small saucepan, combine the sugar, cocoa and flour. Stir in milk until smooth. Add butter. Cook and stir over medium-high heat until thickened and bubbly. Reduce heat; cook and stir 2 minutes longer. Remove from the heat. Stir a small amount of hot filling into eggs; return all to pan, stirring constantly. Fold in half of the pie filling.

2. Pour into pastry shell. Bake at 350° for 35-40 minutes or until filling is almost set. Cool completely on a wire rack. Just before serving, top with remaining pie filling and whipped topping if desired. **Yield:** 6-8 servings.

Cran-Apple Cobbler —Jo Ann Sheehan, Ruther Glen, Virginia

2-1/2 cups sliced peeled apples
2-1/2 cups sliced peeled firm pears
1 to 1-1/4 cups sugar
1 cup fresh *or* frozen cranberries, thawed
1 cup water
3 tablespoons quick-cooking tapioca
3 tablespoons red-hot candies
1/2 teaspoon ground cinnamon
2 tablespoons butter
TOPPING:
3/4 cup all-purpose flour
2 tablespoons sugar
1 teaspoon baking powder
1/4 teaspoon salt
1/4 cup cold butter
3 tablespoons milk
Vanilla ice cream

1. In a large saucepan, combine the first eight ingredients; let stand for 5 minutes. Cook and stir over medium heat until mixture comes to a full rolling boil, about 18 minutes. Transfer cran-apple mixture to a greased 2-qt. baking dish; dot with butter.

2. Combine the flour, sugar, baking powder and salt in a bowl. Cut in butter until mixture resembles coarse crumbs. Stir in milk until a soft dough forms.

3. Drop topping by heaping tablespoonfuls onto hot fruit. Bake at 375° for 30-35 minutes or until golden brown. Serve warm with ice cream. **Yield:** 6-8 servings.

Chocolate Macaroon Cake —Saburo Aburano, Ann Arbor, Michigan

1 egg white
3 tablespoons sugar
2 cups flaked coconut, finely chopped
1 tablespoon all-purpose flour
CAKE BATTER:
4 eggs, *separated*
1-3/4 cups sugar, *divided*
1/2 cup shortening
1/2 cup sour cream
2 teaspoons vanilla extract
1/2 cup brewed coffee
1/4 cup buttermilk
2 cups all-purpose flour
1/2 cup baking cocoa
1 teaspoon baking soda
1 teaspoon salt
FROSTING:
1 cup semisweet chocolate chips, melted and cooled
3 tablespoons butter, softened
2 cups confectioners' sugar
5 tablespoons milk

1. In a small mixing bowl, beat egg white on medium speed until soft peaks form. Gradually beat in sugar, 1 tablespoon at a time, on high until stiff glossy peaks form and sugar is dissolved. Fold in coconut and flour; set aside.

2. In a large mixing bowl, beat the egg whites on medium until soft peaks form. Gradually beat in 1/2 cup sugar, 1 tablespoon at a time, on high until stiff glossy peaks form and sugar is dissolved; set aside. In another mixing bowl, cream shortening and remaining sugar. Add the egg yolks, sour cream and vanilla; beat until creamy. Combine coffee and buttermilk. Combine the flour, cocoa, baking soda and salt; add to creamed mixture alternately with coffee mixture. Beat until combined. Fold in beaten egg whites.

3. Pour half of the batter into an ungreased 10-in. tube pan with removable bottom. Drop the coconut filling by spoonfuls over the batter. Top with remaining batter. Bake at 350° for 55-60 minutes or until a toothpick inserted near the center comes out clean. Immediately invert cake onto a wire rack; cool completely, about 1 hour. Run a knife around side of pan and remove.

4. In a mixing bowl, combine frosting ingredients. Beat until smooth and creamy. Spread over the top and sides of cake. **Yield:** 12-16 servings.

Cran-Apple Cobbler

Gran's Apple Cake —*Lauris Conrad, Turlock, California*

1-2/3 cups sugar
2 eggs
1/2 cup unsweetened applesauce
2 tablespoons canola oil
2 teaspoons vanilla extract
2 cups all-purpose flour
2 teaspoons baking soda
2 teaspoons ground cinnamon
3/4 teaspoon salt
6 cups chopped peeled tart apples
(about 3 medium)
1/2 cup chopped pecans
FROSTING:
4 ounces cream cheese
2 tablespoons butter, softened
1 teaspoon vanilla extract
1 cup confectioners' sugar

1. In a mixing bowl, combine the sugar, eggs, applesauce, oil and vanilla. Beat for 2 minutes on medium speed. Combine the flour, baking soda, cinnamon and salt; add to applesauce mixture and beat until combined. Fold in apples and pecans.

2. Transfer to a 13-in. x 9-in. x 2-in. baking dish coated with nonstick cooking spray. Bake at 350° for 35-40 minutes or until top is golden brown and a toothpick inserted near center comes out clean. Cool on a wire rack.

3. For frosting, combine cream cheese, butter and vanilla in a small mixing bowl until smooth. Gradually beat in confectioners' sugar (mixture will be soft). Spread over cooled cake. **Yield:** 18 servings.

Crustless Pineapple Pie —*Christi Ross, Guthrie, Texas*

2 cups milk
2/3 cup sugar
1/2 cup biscuit/baking mix
1/4 cup butter, melted
2 eggs
1-1/2 teaspoons vanilla extract
Yellow food coloring, optional
2 cans (8 ounces *each*) crushed
pineapple, well drained
Whipped topping, optional

1. In a blender, combine the milk, sugar, biscuit mix, butter, eggs, vanilla and food coloring if desired; cover and process until smooth. Sprinkle the pineapple into a greased deep-dish 9-in. pie plate. Pour batter over pineapple.

2. Bake at 350° for 40-45 minutes or until a knife inserted near the center comes out clean. Garnish with whipped topping if desired. **Yield:** 6-8 servings.

Sky-High Strawberry Pie —*Janet Mooberry, Peoria, Illinois*

3 quarts fresh strawberries, *divided*
1-1/2 cups sugar
6 tablespoons cornstarch
2/3 cup water
Red food coloring, optional
1 deep-dish pastry shell (10 inches),
  baked
1 cup heavy whipping cream
1-1/2 tablespoons instant vanilla pudding
  mix

1. In a large bowl, mash enough berries to equal 3 cups. In a saucepan, combine the sugar and cornstarch. Stir in the mashed berries and water; mix well. Bring to a boil over medium heat; cook and stir for 2 minutes or until thickened. Remove from the heat; add food coloring if desired. Pour into a large bowl. Chill for 20 minutes, stirring occasionally, until mixture is just slightly warm.

2. Fold in the remaining berries. Pile into pie shell. Chill for 2-3 hours.

3. In a small mixing bowl, whip cream until soft peaks form. Sprinkle pudding mix over cream and whip until stiff. Pipe around edge of pie or dollop on individual slices. **Yield:** 8-10 servings.

Pear Apple Crisp —*Judy Foye, Freeport, Maine*

1 can (21 ounces) apple pie filling
1 can (8-1/2 ounces) sliced pears,
  drained
1/2 cup packed brown sugar
1/2 cup all-purpose flour
1/4 cup quick-cooking oats
1/2 teaspoon ground cinnamon
6 tablespoons cold butter
Ice cream, optional

1. In a greased 9-in. baking dish, combine pie filling and pears; set aside. In a small bowl, combine brown sugar, flour, oats and cinnamon; cut in butter until mixture resembles coarse crumbs. Sprinkle over fruit.

2. Bake at 350° for 23-25 minutes or until golden brown. Serve with ice cream if desired. **Yield:** 4 servings.

Chocolate Almond Cake —*Margaret Malinowski, Oak Creek, Wisconsin*

1/3 cup butter, softened
1/3 cup shortening
1-3/4 cups sugar
2 eggs
1-1/2 teaspoons vanilla extract
2 cups all-purpose flour
1/2 cup baking cocoa
1 teaspoon baking powder
1/2 teaspoon baking soda
1/2 teaspoon salt
1-1/4 cups buttermilk
FROSTING:
3 cups heavy whipping cream
1 cup confectioners' sugar
3 tablespoons baking cocoa
1-1/2 teaspoons vanilla extract
6 tablespoons seedless raspberry jam, warmed
1-1/2 to 2 cups sliced almonds, toasted
Fresh raspberries and mint

1. Line two greased 9-in. round baking pans with waxed paper; set aside. In a mixing bowl, cream the butter, shortening and sugar until fluffy. Add eggs, one at a time, beating well after each addition. Add vanilla. Combine the flour, cocoa, baking powder, baking soda and salt. Add to the creamed mixture alternately with the buttermilk; mix well.

2. Pour into prepared pans. Bake at 350° for 25-30 minutes or until a toothpick inserted near the center comes out clean. Cool for 10 minutes before removing from pans to wire racks to cool completely.

3. For frosting, beat cream in a mixing bowl until soft peaks form. Add sugar and cocoa, 2 tablespoons at a time, beating on high until stiff peaks form. Beat in vanilla. Spread about 2 tablespoons jam over each cake layer.

4. Place one cake on a serving plate. Spread with 1-1/2 cups whipped cream mixture; drizzle with remaining jam. Top with remaining cake layer; spread the remaining whipped cream mixture over top and sides of cake. Press almonds onto sides and top of cake. Garnish with raspberries and mint. Store in the refrigerator.
Yield: 12-14 servings.

Pumpkin Apple Pie —*Elizabeth Montogomery, Taylorville, Illinois*

1/3 cup packed brown sugar
1 tablespoon cornstarch
1/2 teaspoon ground cinnamon
1/4 teaspoon salt
1/3 cup water
2 tablespoons butter
3 cups sliced peeled tart apples
Pastry for a single-crust pie (9 inches)
PUMPKIN LAYER:
3/4 cup canned pumpkin
3/4 cup evaporated milk
1/3 cup sugar
1 egg
1/2 teaspoon ground cinnamon
1/4 teaspoon salt
Whipped cream, optional

1. In a saucepan, combine brown sugar, cornstarch, cinnamon and salt. Add water and butter; bring to a boil. Add apples. Cook and stir for 4 minutes. Place pastry in a 9-in. pie pan; add apple mixture.

2. In a bowl, whisk pumpkin, milk, sugar, egg, cinnamon and salt until smooth; pour over apple layer. Flute the edges or decorate with pastry leaves.

3. Bake at 375° for 50-55 minutes or until a knife inserted near the center comes out clean. If necessary, cover edges with foil for the last 15 minutes of baking time to prevent overbrowning. Cool completely. Garnish with whipped cream if desired. Store in the refrigerator. **Yield:** 6-8 servings.

Editor's Note: Additional pastry will be needed to decorate pie with pastry leaves.

Cranberry Sauce Cake —*Marge Clark, West Lebanon, Indiana*

3 cups all-purpose flour
1-1/2 cups sugar
1 cup mayonnaise
1 can (16 ounces) whole-berry cranberry sauce
1/3 cup orange juice
1 tablespoon grated orange peel
1 teaspoon baking soda
1 teaspoon salt
1 teaspoon orange extract
1 cup chopped walnuts
ICING:
1 cup confectioners' sugar
1 to 2 tablespoons orange juice

1. In a mixing bowl, combine flour, sugar, mayonnaise, cranberry sauce, orange juice and peel, baking soda, salt and extract; mix well. Fold in walnuts. Cut waxed or parchment paper to fit the bottom of a 10-in. tube pan. Spray the pan and paper with nonstick cooking spray.

2. Pour batter into paper-lined pan. Bake at 350° for 60-70 minutes or until a toothpick inserted near the center comes out clean. Cool for 10 minutes before removing from pan to a wire rack. Combine icing ingredients; drizzle over the warm cake. **Yield:** 12-16 servings.

Perfect Rhubarb Pie —*Ellen Benninger, Stoneboro, Pennsylvania*

  4 cups sliced fresh rhubarb
  4 cups boiling water
1-1/2 cups sugar
  3 tablespoons all-purpose flour
  1 teaspoon quick-cooking tapioca
  1 egg
  2 teaspoons cold water
Pastry for double-crust pie (9 inches)
  1 tablespoon butter

1. Place rhubarb in a colander and pour water over it; set aside. In a bowl, combine sugar, flour and tapioca. Add rhubarb; toss to coat. Let stand for 15 minutes. Beat egg and water; add to rhubarb mixture and mix well.

2. Line a 9-in. pie plate with bottom pastry. Add filling. Dot with butter. Cover with remaining pastry; flute edges. Cut slits in top crust. Bake at 400° for 15 minutes. Reduce heat to 350°; bake 40-50 minutes longer or until crust is golden brown and filling is bubbly. **Yield:** 8 servings.

Chocolate Mint Layer Cake —*Jean Portwine, Recluse, Wisconsin*

1/2 cup butter, softened
1-3/4 cups sugar
  3 eggs
  4 squares (1 ounce *each*) unsweetened chocolate, melted and cooled
  1 teaspoon vanilla extract
3/4 cup milk
1/2 cup water
1-3/4 cups all-purpose flour
3/4 teaspoon baking soda
1/2 teaspoon salt
FILLING:
  1 cup heavy whipping cream
  3 tablespoons confectioners' sugar
1/8 teaspoon peppermint extract
  3 to 4 drops green food coloring, optional
ICING:
  1 cup (6 ounces) semisweet chocolate chips
1/4 cup butter
1/3 cup evaporated milk
  1 teaspoon vanilla extract
1-1/2 cups confectioners' sugar

1. Line two greased 9-in. round baking pans with waxed paper. Grease and flour the paper; set aside. In a mixing bowl, cream the butter and sugar. Add the eggs, one at a time, beating well after each addition. Beat in chocolate and vanilla.

2. Combine milk and water. Combine the flour, baking soda and salt; add to creamed mixture alternately with milk mixture. Pour into prepared pans. Bake at 350° for 24-28 minutes or until a toothpick comes out clean. Cool for 10 minutes before removing from pans to wire racks.

3. For filling, in a mixing bowl, beat the cream until it begins to thicken. Add confectioners' sugar and extract; beat until stiff peaks form. Beat in food coloring if desired. Place one cake layer on a serving plate; spread with filling. Top with second cake.

4. For icing, in a microwave-safe mixing bowl, melt chips and butter; cool slightly. Beat in evaporated milk and vanilla. Gradually beat in confectioners' sugar. Frost and decorate cake. Chill 2 hours before slicing. **Yield:** 12 servings.

Perfect Rhubarb Pie

Danish Cherry Rhubarb Dessert —*Joan Kallhoff, O'Neill, Nebraska*

2-1/2 cups all-purpose flour
   1 teaspoon salt
   1 cup cold butter
 1/2 cup milk
   1 egg, *separated*
   1 cup cornflakes
  4 to 5 cups diced fresh *or* frozen
     rhubarb, thawed
1-1/2 cups plus 1 tablespoon sugar, *divided*
   1 can (21 ounces) cherry pie filling
   1 teaspoon vanilla extract
GLAZE:
 1/2 cup confectioners' sugar
 1/4 teaspoon vanilla extract
1-1/2 to 2 teaspoons milk

1. In a bowl, combine the flour and salt; cut in butter until crumbly. Add the milk and egg yolk; mix well. Divide in half. On a lightly floured surface, roll each portion into a 13-in. x 9-in. rectangle. Place one rectangle in a greased 13-in. x 9-in. x 2-in. baking dish. Sprinkle with cornflakes.

2. In a bowl, combine the rhubarb and 1-1/2 cups sugar. Stir in the pie filling and vanilla; spread over cornflakes. Top with the remaining pastry. Cut slits in the top. Beat egg white; brush over pastry. Sprinkle with remaining sugar. Bake at 350° for 50-55 minutes or until crust is golden brown. Cool on a wire rack.

3. In a bowl, combine glaze ingredients; drizzle over bars. Store in the refrigerator. **Yield:** 12-16 servings.

   Editor's Note: If using frozen rhubarb, measure rhubarb while still frozen, then thaw completely. Drain in a colander, but do not press liquid out.

Blueberry Upside-Down Cake —*Charlotte Harrison, North Providence, Rhode Island*

   6 tablespoons butter, softened, *divided*
 1/4 cup packed brown sugar
   2 cups fresh blueberries
 3/4 cup sugar
   1 egg
   1 teaspoon vanilla extract
1-1/4 cups cake flour
1-1/2 teaspoons baking powder
 1/2 cup milk
Whipped topping, optional

1. In a small saucepan, melt 2 tablespoons butter; stir in brown sugar. Spread into an ungreased 8-in. baking dish. Arrange blueberries in a single layer over brown sugar mixture; set aside. In a large mixing bowl, cream remaining butter; beat in sugar. Add egg and vanilla; mix well. Combine flour and baking powder; add to creamed mixture alternately with milk. Carefully pour over blueberries.

2. Bake at 350° for 40-45 minutes or until a toothpick inserted near the center of cake comes out clean. Immediately invert onto a serving platter. Cool. Serve with whipped topping if desired. **Yield:** 6-8 servings.

Apple Blackberry Pie –Dorian Lucas, Corning, California

2 cups all-purpose flour
1 teaspoon sugar
1 teaspoon salt
1 teaspoon ground cinnamon
2/3 cup cold butter
4 to 6 tablespoons cold water

FILLING:
5 cups thinly sliced peeled tart apples
  (about 6 medium)
1 cup fresh blackberries
1/2 cup packed brown sugar
4-1/2 teaspoons cornstarch
1 teaspoon ground cinnamon
1 teaspoon ground nutmeg

1. In a bowl, combine the flour, sugar, salt and cinnamon; cut in butter until crumbly. Gradually add water, tossing with a fork until dough forms a ball. Divide dough in half. Roll out one portion to fit a 9-in. pie plate; place pastry in plate and trim even with edge.

2. In a bowl, combine apples and blackberries. Combine the brown sugar, cornstarch, cinnamon and nutmeg; add to fruit mixture and toss to coat. Pour into crust. Roll out remaining pastry to fit top of pie; place over filling. Trim, seal and flute edges. Cut slits in pastry. Add decorative cutouts if desired. Cover edges loosely with foil.

3. Bake at 450° for 10 minutes. Reduce heat to 350°; remove foil. Bake 40-50 minutes longer or until lightly browned and filling is bubbly. Cool on a wire rack. Store in the refrigerator. **Yield:** 6-8 servings.

One-Bowl Chocolate Cake –Coleen Martin, Brookfield, Wisconsin

2 cups all-purpose flour
2 cups sugar
1/2 cup baking cocoa
2 teaspoons baking soda
1 teaspoon baking powder
1/2 teaspoon salt
1 cup vegetable oil
1 cup buttermilk
2 eggs
1 cup hot water
Frosting of your choice
Colored sprinkles, optional

1. In a large bowl, combine dry ingredients. Stir in oil, buttermilk and eggs. Add water and stir until combined.

2. Pour into a greased 13-in. x 9-in. x 2-in. baking pan. Bake at 350° for 35-38 minutes or until a toothpick inserted near the center comes out clean. Cool completely. Frost. Decorate with sprinkles if desired. **Yield:** 12-16 servings.

Old-Fashioned Carrot Cake –*Kim Orr, Louisville, Kentucky*

4 eggs
2 cups sugar
1 cup vegetable oil
2 cups all-purpose flour
2 to 3 teaspoons ground cinnamon
3/4 teaspoon baking soda
1/2 teaspoon baking powder
1/4 teaspoon salt
1/4 teaspoon ground nutmeg
2 cups grated carrots
FROSTING:
1/2 cup butter, softened
1 package (3 ounces) cream cheese, softened
1 teaspoon vanilla extract
3-3/4 cups confectioners' sugar
2 to 3 tablespoons milk
1 cup chopped walnuts
Carrot curls and additional walnuts, optional

1. In a mixing bowl, combine eggs, sugar and oil. Combine flour, cinnamon, baking soda, baking powder, salt and nutmeg; beat into egg mixture. Stir in carrots.

2. Pour into two greased and floured 9-in. round baking pans. Bake at 350° for 35-40 minutes or until a toothpick inserted near the center comes out clean. Cool for 10 minutes before removing from pans to wire racks to cool completely.

3. For frosting, in a mixing bowl, cream butter and cream cheese. Beat in vanilla. Gradually beat in confectioners' sugar. Add enough milk to achieve desired spreading consistency. Stir in walnuts.

4. Spread frosting between layers and over top and sides of cake. Garnish with carrot curls and walnuts if desired. Refrigerate leftovers. **Yield:** 12 servings.

Apple Brown Betty –*Florence Palmer, Marshall, Illinois*

4 slices white bread, toasted
3 cups sliced peeled baking apples
1/2 cup sugar
1/2 cup packed brown sugar
1 teaspoon ground cinnamon
1/4 cup butter, melted
1/2 cup half-and-half cream

1. Tear toast into bite-size pieces; place in a greased 1-1/2-qt. casserole. Top with apples. Combine sugars and cinnamon; sprinkle over apples. Drizzle with butter.

2. Cover and bake at 350° for 1 hour, stirring after 30 minutes. Serve warm with cream. **Yield:** 4 servings.

Brownies & Bars

Cinnamon Brownies —*Christopher Wolf, Belvidere, Illinois*

1-2/3 cups sugar
  3/4 cup butter, melted
    2 tablespoons strong brewed coffee
    2 eggs
    2 teaspoons vanilla extract
1-1/3 cups all-purpose flour
  3/4 cup baking cocoa
    1 tablespoon ground cinnamon
1/2 teaspoon baking powder
1/4 teaspoon salt
    1 cup chopped walnuts
Confectioners' sugar

1. In a mixing bowl, beat the sugar, butter and coffee. Add eggs and vanilla. Combine the flour, cocoa, cinnamon, baking powder and salt; gradually add to the sugar mixture and mix well. Stir in walnuts.

2. Spread into a greased 13-in. x 9-in. x 2-in. baking pan. Bake at 350° for 18-22 minutes or until a toothpick inserted near the center comes out clean (do not overbake). Cool on a wire rack. Dust with confectioners' sugar. **Yield:** 2 dozen.

Pear Custard Bars —*Jeannette Nord, San Juan Capistrano, California*

1/2 cup butter, softened
1/3 cup sugar
3/4 cup all-purpose flour
1/4 teaspoon vanilla extract
2/3 cup chopped macadamia nuts
FILLING/TOPPING:
   1 package (8 ounces) cream cheese, softened
1/2 cup sugar
   1 egg
1/2 teaspoon vanilla extract
   1 can (15-1/4 ounces) pear halves, drained
1/2 teaspoon sugar
1/2 teaspoon ground cinnamon

1. In a mixing bowl, cream butter and sugar. Beat in the flour and vanilla until combined. Stir in the nuts. Press into a greased 8-in. square baking pan. Bake at 350° for 20 minutes or until lightly browned. Cool on a wire rack. Increase heat to 375°.

2. In a mixing bowl, beat cream cheese until smooth. Add sugar, egg and vanilla; mix until combined. Pour over crust. Cut pears into 1/8-in. slices; arrange in a single layer over filling. Combine sugar and cinnamon; sprinkle over pears. Bake at 375° for 28-30 minutes (center will be soft set and will become firmer upon cooling). Cool on a wire rack for 45 minutes. Cover and refrigerate for at least 2 hours before cutting. Store in the refrigerator. **Yield:** 16 bars.

Caramel-Chocolate Oat Squares —*Kellie Ochsner, Newton, Iowa*

3/4 cup butter
1-1/4 cups all-purpose flour
1-1/4 cups quick-cooking oats
3/4 cup packed brown sugar
1/2 teaspoon baking soda
1/4 teaspoon salt
 24 caramels
1/4 cup milk
   1 cup (6 ounces) semisweet chocolate chips
1/2 cup chopped walnuts, optional

1. In a microwave-safe bowl, heat butter, uncovered, on high for 30-45 seconds or until softened. Combine flour, oats, brown sugar, baking soda and salt; stir into butter until blended. Set a third of the mixture aside for topping.

2. Press remaining mixture into an 8-in. square microwave-safe dish. Cook, uncovered, on high for 2-3 minutes or until crust is raised and set (crust will be uneven), rotating a half turn after each minute.

3. In a 1-qt. microwave-safe dish, heat the caramels and milk, uncovered, on high for 3-4 minutes or until melted and smooth, stirring every minute. Sprinkle chips and nuts if desired over crust. Pour caramel mixture over all. Sprinkle with reserved oat mixture; press down lightly. Microwave, uncovered, on high for 3-4 minutes or until the caramel is bubbly, rotating a quarter turn every minute. Cool before cutting. **Yield:** 16 servings.

Editor's Note: This recipe was tested in an 850-watt microwave.

White Brownies —*Geneva Mayer, Olney, Illinois*

6 squares (1 ounce *each*) white baking
  chocolate
1 cup butter
6 eggs
3 cups sugar
2 teaspoons vanilla extract
3 cups all-purpose flour
1 teaspoon baking powder
1/2 teaspoon salt
1 package (10 to 12 ounces) vanilla *or*
  white chips
1 cup chopped pecans

1. In a microwave or heavy saucepan, melt chocolate and butter; cool for 20 minutes.

2. In a mixing bowl, beat eggs and sugar until thick and lemon-colored, about 4 minutes. Gradually beat in melted chocolate and vanilla. Combine flour, baking powder and salt; add to chocolate mixture. Stir in chips and pecans.

3. Pour into a greased 15-in. x 10-in. x 1-in. baking pan. Bake at 350° for 40-45 minutes or until golden brown. Cool on a wire rack. **Yield:** about 4 dozen.

PB&J Bars —*Mitzi Sentiff, Alexandria, Virginia*

1 package (18 ounces) refrigerated
  sugar cookie dough, *divided*
2/3 cup strawberry jam
3/4 cup granola cereal without raisins
3/4 cup peanut butter chips

1. Line a 9-in. square baking pan with foil and grease the foil. Press two-thirds of the cookie dough into prepared pan. Spread jam over dough to within 1/4 in. of edges. In a mixing bowl, beat the granola, peanut butter chips and remaining dough until blended. Crumble over jam.

2. Bake at 375° for 25-30 minutes or until golden brown. Cool on a wire rack. Using foil, lift out of pan. Cut into bars and remove from foil. **Yield:** 9-12 servings.

Chocolate Chip Cheesecake Bars —Jane Nolt, Narvon, Pennsylvania

3/4 cup shortening
3/4 cup sugar
1/3 cup packed brown sugar
1 egg
1-1/2 teaspoons vanilla extract
1-1/2 cups all-purpose flour
1 teaspoon salt
3/4 teaspoon baking soda
1-1/2 cups miniature chocolate chips
3/4 cup chopped pecans

FILLING:
2 packages (8 ounces *each*) cream cheese, softened
3/4 cup sugar
2 eggs
1 teaspoon vanilla extract

1. In a mixing bowl, cream shortening and sugars. Beat in egg and vanilla. Combine the flour, salt and baking soda; add to the creamed mixture and mix well. Fold in the chocolate chips and pecans. Set aside a third of the dough for topping. Press remaining dough into a greased 13-in. x 9-in. x 2-in. baking pan. Bake at 350° for 8 minutes.

2. Meanwhile, in a small mixing bowl, beat cream cheese and sugar until smooth. Add eggs and vanilla; mix well. Spoon over crust. Drop teaspoonfuls of reserved dough over filling. Bake at 350° for 35-40 minutes or until golden brown. Cool on a wire rack. Cover and store in the refrigerator. **Yield:** 3 dozen.

Peppermint Brownies —Marcy Greenblatt, Redding, California

3/4 cup vegetable oil
2 cups sugar
2 teaspoons vanilla extract
4 eggs
1-1/3 cups all-purpose flour
1 cup baking cocoa
1 teaspoon baking powder
1 teaspoon salt
3/4 cup crushed peppermint candy, *divided*

GLAZE:
1 cup (6 ounces) semisweet chocolate chips
1 tablespoon shortening

1. Line a 13-in. x 9-in. x 2-in. baking pan with foil; grease the foil and set aside. In a mixing bowl, beat oil and sugar. Stir in vanilla. Add eggs, one at a time, beating well after each addition. Combine the flour, cocoa, baking powder and salt; gradually add to creamed mixture. Set aside 2 tablespoons peppermint candy for garnish; stir remaining candy into creamed mixture. Spread into prepared pan.

2. Bake at 350° for 35-40 minutes or until a toothpick inserted near the center comes out clean. Cool on a wire rack.

3. For glaze, melt chocolate chips and shortening in a microwave or heavy saucepan; stir until smooth. Spread over brownies; sprinkle with reserved candy. **Yield:** 2 dozen.

Chocolate Chip Cheesecake Bars

Lemon Cheesecake Squares –Peggy Reddick, Cumming, Georgia

3/4 cup shortening
1/3 cup packed brown sugar
1-1/4 cups all-purpose flour
1 cup old-fashioned oats
1/4 teaspoon salt
1/2 cup seedless raspberry jam
FILLING:
4 packages (8 ounces *each*) cream cheese, softened
1-1/2 cups sugar
1/4 cup all-purpose flour
4 eggs
1/3 cup lemon juice
4 teaspoons grated lemon peel

1. In a mixing bowl, cream shortening and brown sugar. Combine the flour, oats and salt; gradually add to creamed mixture. Press dough into a greased 13-in. x 9-in. x 2-in. baking dish. Bake at 350° for 15-18 minutes or until golden brown. Spread with jam.

2. For filling, beat the cream cheese, sugar and flour until fluffy. Add the eggs, lemon juice and peel just until blended. Carefully spoon over jam. Bake at 350° for 30-35 minutes or until center is almost set. Cool on a wire rack. Cover and store in the refrigerator. **Yield:** 20 servings.

Cranberry Popcorn Bars –Steve Dold, Monon, Indiana

6 cups popped popcorn
3 cups miniature marshmallows
1 tablespoon butter
1 cup dried cranberries, chopped
1 cup chopped walnuts
2 tablespoons grated orange peel
1/4 teaspoon salt

1. Place popcorn in a large bowl; set aside. In a heavy saucepan over low heat, cook and stir marshmallows and butter until smooth. Stir in cranberries, walnuts, orange peel and salt; mix well.

2. Pour over popcorn and toss to coat. Press into a greased 11-in. x 7-in. x 2-in. baking pan. Cool. Cut into bars with a serrated knife. **Yield:** 1 dozen.

Candy Bar Brownies —*Sharon Evans, Rockwell, Iowa*

3/4 cup butter, melted
2 cups sugar
4 eggs
2 teaspoons vanilla extract
1-1/2 cups all-purpose flour
1/3 cup baking cocoa
1/2 teaspoon baking powder
1/4 teaspoon salt
4 Snickers bars (2.07 ounces *each*), cut into 1/4-inch pieces
3 plain milk chocolate candy bars (1.55 ounces *each*), coarsely chopped

1. In a bowl, combine butter, sugar, eggs and vanilla. Combine flour, cocoa, baking powder and salt; set aside 1/4 cup. Add remaining dry ingredients to the egg mixture; mix well. Toss Snickers pieces with reserved flour mixture; stir into batter.

2. Transfer to a greased 13-in. x 9-in. x 2-in. baking pan. Sprinkle with milk chocolate candy bar pieces. Bake at 350° for 30-35 minutes or until a toothpick inserted near the center comes out clean (do not overbake). Cool on a wire rack. Chill before cutting. **Yield:** 3 dozen.

Crunchy Peanut Butter Bars —*Geraldine Grisdale, Mt. Pleasant, Michigan*

2-3/4 cups all-purpose flour
1-1/4 cups packed brown sugar
1 egg
1/2 cup butter, softened
1/2 cup shortening
1/3 cup chunky peanut butter
1 teaspoon vanilla extract
1/2 teaspoon salt
TOPPING:
1 cup (6 ounces) semisweet chocolate chips, melted
1/2 cup chunky peanut butter
1-1/2 cups crushed cornflakes

1. In a mixing bowl, combine the first eight ingredients and mix well (batter will be thick). Press into an ungreased 15-in. x 10-in. x 1-in. baking pan. Bake at 350° for 15-20 minutes or until set. Cool for 5 minutes.

2. Meanwhile, combine chocolate chips and peanut butter in a bowl; stir in cornflakes. Carefully spread on top. Cut into bars. **Yield:** 4 dozen.

Dark Chocolate Mocha Brownies –*Linda McCoy, Oostburg, Wisconsin*

  2 cups packed brown sugar
  1 cup butter, melted
  3 eggs
  1 tablespoon instant coffee granules
  2 teaspoons vanilla extract
  1 cup all-purpose flour
  1 cup baking cocoa
1/2 teaspoon baking powder
1/2 teaspoon salt
  6 ounces bittersweet chocolate, coarsely chopped
FROSTING:
1/4 cup butter, melted
  3 tablespoons sour cream
  2 teaspoons vanilla extract
2-3/4 to 3 cups confectioners' sugar
  2 ounces grated bittersweet chocolate

1. In a mixing bowl, combine brown sugar and butter. Beat in eggs, one at a time. Add coffee and vanilla; mix well. Combine the flour, cocoa, baking powder and salt; add to sugar mixture and mix well. Stir in chocolate.

2. Spread into a greased 13-in. x 9-in. x 2-in. baking pan. Bake at 350° for 25-30 minutes or until a toothpick inserted near the center comes out clean. Cool on a wire rack.

3. For frosting, combine butter, sour cream and vanilla. Gradually stir in sugar until frosting is smooth and reaches desired consistency. Frost brownies. Sprinkle with grated chocolate. **Yield:** 5 dozen.

Ribbon-o-Fudge Popcorn Bars —Flo Burtnett, Gage, Oklahoma

2 cups (12 ounces) semisweet chocolate chips
2 tablespoons shortening
3 tablespoons butter
4 cups miniature marshmallows
1 cup butterscotch chips
3 quarts popped popcorn

1. In a microwave or double boiler, melt chocolate chips and shortening. Chill for 15-20 minutes or until thickened.

2. Meanwhile, line a 9-in. square baking pan with foil; grease the foil and set pan aside. In a heavy saucepan over low heat, melt butter. Stir in marshmallows and butterscotch chips until melted and smooth.

3. Place the popcorn in a large bowl; add marshmallow mixture and toss until coated. Firmly press half of the popcorn mixture into prepared pan. Spread chocolate mixture evenly over popcorn. Firmly press remaining popcorn mixture over chocolate. Chill for 30 minutes. Lift out of pan, using foil edges. Remove foil; cut into bars. **Yield:** 2 dozen.

Fruit Cocktail Bars —Linda Tackman, Escanaba, Michigan

1-1/2 cups sugar
2 eggs
1 can (17 ounces) fruit cocktail, undrained
1 teaspoon vanilla extract
2-1/4 cups all-purpose flour
1-1/2 teaspoons baking soda
1 teaspoon salt
1-1/3 cups flaked coconut
1 cup chopped walnuts
GLAZE:
1/2 cup sugar
1/4 cup butter
2 tablespoons milk
1/4 teaspoon vanilla extract

1. In a mixing bowl, cream sugar and eggs. Add fruit cocktail and vanilla; mix well. Combine the flour, baking soda and salt; add to the creamed mixture and mix well.

2. Pour into a greased 15-in. x 10-in. x 1-in. baking pan. Sprinkle with coconut and walnuts.

Bake at 350° for 20-25 minutes or until a toothpick comes out clean. Cool for 10 minutes.

3. In a saucepan, bring sugar, butter and milk to a boil. Remove from the heat; add vanilla and mix well. Drizzle over cake. Cool. Cut into bars. **Yield:** 2 to 2-1/2 dozen.

Crimson Crumble Bars —*Paula Eriksen, Palm Harbor, Florida*

1 cup sugar
2 teaspoons cornstarch
2 cups fresh *or* frozen cranberries
1 can (8 ounces) unsweetened crushed
   pineapple, undrained
1 cup all-purpose flour
2/3 cup old-fashioned oats
2/3 cup packed brown sugar
1/4 teaspoon salt
1/2 cup cold butter
1/2 cup chopped pecans

1. In a saucepan, combine the sugar, cornstarch, cranberries and pineapple; bring to a boil, stirring often. Reduce heat; cover and simmer for 10-15 minutes or until the berries pop. Remove from the heat.

2. In a large bowl, combine the flour, oats, brown sugar and salt. Cut in butter until mixture resembles coarse crumbs. Stir in pecans. Set aside 1-1/2 cups for topping. Press remaining crumb mixture onto the bottom of a 13-in. x 9-in. x 2-in. baking pan coated with nonstick cooking spray. Bake at 350° for 8-10 minutes or until firm; cool for 10 minutes.

3. Pour fruit filling over crust. Sprinkle with reserved crumb mixture. Bake for 25-30 minutes or until golden brown. Cool on a wire rack. **Yield:** 2 dozen.

Cappuccino Truffle Brownies —*Karen Yetter, Oceanside, California*

2 squares (1 ounce *each*) semisweet
   chocolate
1/2 cup butter
2 eggs
3/4 cup packed brown sugar
1 teaspoon vanilla extract
3/4 cup all-purpose flour
1/2 teaspoon baking powder
1/2 teaspoon ground cinnamon
FILLING:
1 package (8 ounces) cream cheese,
   softened
1/4 cup confectioners' sugar
1 teaspoon instant coffee granules
1 tablespoon hot water
1 cup (6 ounces) semisweet chocolate
   chips
1/2 teaspoon butter
GLAZE:
1/2 cup semisweet chocolate chips
1 teaspoon shortening
Whole blanched almonds

1. In a heavy saucepan or microwave, melt chocolate and butter; stir until smooth. Cool slightly. In a small mixing bowl, beat eggs, brown sugar and vanilla. Beat in chocolate mixture. Combine the flour, baking powder and cinnamon; stir into chocolate mixture. Spread into a greased 9-in. square baking pan. Bake at 350° for 20-22 minutes or until toothpick comes out clean. Cool on a wire rack.

2. For filling, in a mixing bowl, beat the cream cheese and confectioners' sugar until light and fluffy. Dissolve coffee in water. Stir into cream cheese mixture. In a heavy saucepan or microwave, melt chips and butter; stir until smooth. Add to cream cheese mixture; beat well. Spread over brownies.

3. For glaze, in a heavy saucepan or microwave, melt chips and butter; stir until smooth. Dip each almond halfway into glaze and place on a waxed paper-lined baking sheet. Let stand until chocolate is set. Drizzle remaining glaze over bars. Place almond in the center of each bar. Refrigerate leftovers. **Yield:** 16 bars.

Crimson Crumble Bars

Cookies 'n' Cream Brownies —*Darlene Brenden, Salem, Oregon*

CREAM CHEESE LAYER:
- 1 package (8 ounces) cream cheese, softened
- 1/4 cup sugar
- 1 egg
- 1/2 teaspoon vanilla extract

BROWNIE LAYER:
- 1/2 cup butter, melted
- 1/2 cup sugar
- 1/2 cup packed brown sugar
- 1/2 cup baking cocoa
- 2 eggs
- 1/2 cup all-purpose flour
- 1 teaspoon baking powder
- 1 teaspoon vanilla extract
- 12 cream-filled chocolate sandwich cookies, crushed

1. In a small mixing bowl, beat the cream cheese, sugar, egg and vanilla until smooth; set aside.

2. For brownie layer, combine butter, sugars and cocoa in a large mixing bowl; blend well. Add eggs, one at a time, beating well after each addition. Combine flour and baking powder; stir into the cocoa mixture. Stir in vanilla and cookie crumbs. Pour into a greased 11-in. x 7-in. x 2-in. baking pan.

3. Spoon cream cheese mixture over batter; cut through batter with a knife to swirl. Bake at 350° for 25-30 minutes or until a toothpick inserted near the center comes out with moist crumbs. Cool completely. **Yield:** 2 dozen.

Classic Lemon Bars —*Melissa Mosness, Loveland, Colorado*

- 1/2 cup butter, softened
- 1/4 cup sugar
- 1 cup all-purpose flour

FILLING:
- 2 eggs
- 3/4 cup sugar
- 3 tablespoons lemon juice
- 2 tablespoons all-purpose flour
- 1/4 teaspoon baking powder

Confectioners' sugar

1. In a small mixing bowl, cream the butter and sugar; gradually add the flour. Press into an ungreased 8-in. square baking dish. Bake at 375° for 12 minutes. Cool slightly.

2. Meanwhile, in another mixing bowl, beat the eggs, sugar, lemon juice, flour and baking powder until frothy. Pour over warm crust. Bake for 15-20 minutes or until lightly browned. Cool on a wire rack. Dust with confectioners' sugar. Cut into bars. **Yield:** 9 servings.

S'mores Bars —*Kristine Brown, Rio Rancho, New Mexico*

8 to 10 whole graham crackers
  (about 5 inches x 2-1/2 inches)
1 package fudge brownie mix
  (13-inch x 9-inch pan size)
2 cups miniature marshmallows
1 cup (6 ounces) semisweet chocolate
  chips
2/3 cup chopped peanuts

1. Arrange graham crackers in a single layer in a greased 13-in. x 9-in. x 2-in. baking pan. Prepare the brownie batter according to package directions. Spread over crackers. Bake at 350° for 25-30 minutes or until a toothpick inserted near the center comes out clean.

2. Sprinkle with marshmallows, chocolate chips and peanuts. Bake 5 minutes longer or until marshmallows are slightly puffed and golden brown. Cool on a wire rack before cutting. **Yield:** 2 dozen.

Scandinavian Almond Bars —*Melva Baumer, Millmont, Pennsylvania*

1/2 cup butter, softened
1 cup sugar
1 egg
1/2 teaspoon almond extract
1-3/4 cups all-purpose flour
2 teaspoons baking powder
1/4 teaspoon salt
1 tablespoon milk
1/2 cup sliced almonds, chopped
ICING:
1 cup confectioners' sugar
1/4 teaspoon almond extract
1 to 2 tablespoons milk

1. In a mixing bowl, cream butter and sugar; beat in egg and extract. Combine dry ingredients; add to creamed mixture and mix well. Divide dough into fourths; form into 12-in. x 3-in. rectangles. Place 5 in. apart on greased baking sheets. Brush with milk; sprinkle with almonds.

2. Bake at 325° for 18-20 minutes or until firm to the touch and edges are lightly browned. Cool on pans for 5 minutes, then cut diagonally into 1-in. slices. Remove to wire racks to cool completely. Combine icing ingredients; drizzle over bars. **Yield:** about 4 dozen.

Raspberry Nut Bars —*Beth Ask, Ulster, Pennsylvania*

1/2 cup margarine
1/4 cup margarine
1/3 cup packed brown sugar
1/4 cup sugar
1 egg
1 teaspoon vanilla extract
2 cups all-purpose flour
1 teaspoon baking powder
1/4 teaspoon baking soda
1/4 teaspoon salt
3/4 cup chopped pecans, *divided*
2/3 cup raspberry jam
2 tablespoons lemon juice
GLAZE:
1/2 cup confectioners' sugar
2 teaspoons milk

1. In a mixing bowl, cream margarines and sugars. Beat in egg and vanilla. Combine flour, baking powder, baking soda and salt; add to creamed mixture and mix well. Stir in 1/2 cup pecans.

2. Spread half of the dough into a 13-in. x 9-in. x 2-in. baking pan coated with nonstick cooking spray. Combine jam and lemon juice; spread over dough. Dollop remaining dough over top. Sprinkle with remaining pecans.

3. Bake at 325° for 30-35 minutes or until lightly browned. Cool. Combine glaze ingredients; drizzle over bars. **Yield:** 3 dozen.

Editor's Note: This recipe uses both regular margarine and reduced-fat margarine.

Blond Toffee Brownies –*Mary Williams, Lancaster, California*

1/2 cup butter, softened
1 cup sugar
1/2 cup packed brown sugar
2 eggs
1 teaspoon vanilla extract
1-1/2 cups all-purpose flour
2 teaspoons baking powder
1/4 teaspoon salt
1 cup English toffee bits *or* almond brickle chips

1. In a mixing bowl, cream butter and sugars. Add eggs, one at a time, beating well after each addition. Beat in vanilla. Combine the flour, baking powder and salt; gradually add to creamed mixture. Stir in toffee bits.

2. Spread evenly into a greased 13-in. x 9-in. x 2-in. baking pan. Bake at 350° for 35-40 minutes or until a toothpick inserted near the center comes out clean. Cool on a wire rack. Cut into bars. **Yield:** 1-1/2 dozen.

Can't Leave Alone Bars –*Kimberly Biel, Java, South Dakota*

1 package (18-1/4 ounces) white cake mix
2 eggs
1/3 cup vegetable oil
1 can (14 ounces) sweetened condensed milk
1 cup (6 ounces) semisweet chocolate chips
1/4 cup butter, cubed

1. In a bowl, combine the dry cake mix, eggs and oil. With floured hands, press two-thirds of the mixture into a greased 13-in. x 9-in. x 2-in. baking pan. Set remaining cake mixture aside.

2. In a microwave-safe bowl, combine the milk, chocolate chips and butter. Microwave, uncovered, on high for 45 seconds; stir. Microwave 45-60 seconds longer or until chips and butter are melted; stir until smooth. Pour over crust.

3. Drop teaspoonfuls of remaining cake mixture over top. Bake at 350° for 20-25 minutes or until lightly browned. Cool before cutting. **Yield:** 3 dozen.

Editor's Note: This recipe was tested in an 850-watt microwave.

Orange Cheesecake Bars —*Connie Faulkner, Moxee, Washington*

2 cups crushed vanilla wafers (about 40)
1/4 cup butter, melted
3 packages (8 ounces *each*) cream cheese, softened
1 can (14 ounces) sweetened condensed milk
3 eggs
2 teaspoons vanilla extract
2 tablespoons orange juice concentrate
1 teaspoon grated orange peel
1 teaspoon orange extract
5 drops yellow food coloring
3 drops red food coloring

1. In a bowl, combine the wafer crumbs and butter. Press into a greased 13-in. x 9-in. x 2-in. baking pan. In a mixing bowl, beat cream cheese until smooth. Add the milk, eggs and vanilla; beat just until combined. Pour half over crust.

2. Add the orange juice concentrate, orange peel, extract and food coloring to the remaining cream cheese mixture; beat until combined. Pour over first layer. Bake at 325° for 45-50 minutes or until center is almost set. Cool on a wire rack. Refrigerate for at least 2 hours before cutting. **Yield:** 3 dozen.

Graham Cracker Brownies —*Cathy Guffey, Towanda, Pennsylvania*

2 cups graham cracker crumbs (about 32 squares)
1 cup (6 ounces) semisweet chocolate chips
1 teaspoon baking powder
Dash salt
1 can (14 ounces) sweetened condensed milk

In a bowl, combine all the ingredients. Spread into a greased 8-in. square baking pan. Bake at 350° for 30-35 minutes or until a toothpick inserted near the center comes out clean. Cool on a wire rack. **Yield:** 1-1/2 dozen.

Chocolate Peanut Butter Bars —*Lorrie Speer, Centralia, Washington*

1 cup sugar
1 cup light corn syrup
1 cup peanut butter
6 cups crisp rice cereal
2 cups (12 ounces) semisweet chocolate chips, melted

1. In a large saucepan, combine the sugar, corn syrup and peanut butter. Cook over medium-low heat until the sugar is dissolved. Remove from the heat; add cereal and stir until coated.

2. Spread into a greased 13-in. x 9-in. x 2-in. pan; press lightly. Spread melted chocolate over bars. Chill. **Yield:** 1-1/2 to 2 dozen.

Orange Cheesecake Bars

Almond Fruit Squares –Iola Egle, McCook, Nebraska

2 tubes (8 ounces *each*) refrigerated
  crescent rolls
3 tablespoons sugar, *divided*
1 package (8 ounces) cream cheese,
  softened
1/3 cup almond paste
1/2 teaspoon almond extract
2 cups halved fresh strawberries
1 can (11 ounces) mandarin oranges,
  drained
1 cup fresh raspberries
1 cup halved green grapes
2 kiwifruit, peeled, quartered and sliced
1/2 cup apricot preserves, warmed
1/2 cup slivered almonds, toasted

Unroll crescent dough and separate into eight rectangles. Place in an ungreased 15-in. x 10-in. x 1-in. baking pan. Press onto bottom and up sides; seal seams and perforations. Sprinkle with 1 tablespoon sugar. Bake at 375° for 14-16 minutes or until golden brown. Cool.

2. In a mixing bowl, beat cream cheese, almond paste, extract and remaining sugar until smooth. Spread over crust. Top with fruit. Brush with preserves; sprinkle with almonds. **Yield:** 16 servings.

Polka-Dot Cookie Bars –Elizabeth Poire, Kailua-Kona, Hawaii

1 cup butter, softened
3/4 cup sugar
3/4 cup packed brown sugar
2 eggs
1/2 teaspoon almond extract
2-1/4 cups all-purpose flour
1/3 cup baking cocoa
1 teaspoon baking soda
1/2 teaspoon salt
1 package (10 to 12 ounces) vanilla *or*
  white chips, *divided*

1. In a mixing bowl, cream butter and sugars. Add eggs, one at a time, beating well after each addition. Beat in extract. Combine flour, cocoa, baking soda and salt; gradually add to the creamed mixture. Set aside 1/4 cup vanilla chips; stir remaining chips into batter.

2. Spread in a greased 15-in. x 10-in. x 1-in. baking pan. Sprinkle with reserved chips. Bake at 375° for 18-23 minutes or until a toothpick inserted near the center comes out clean. Cool before cutting. **Yield:** 4 dozen.

Chocolate-Dipped Brownies —*Jackie Archer, Clinton, Iowa*

    3/4 **cup sugar**
    1/3 **cup butter**
      2 **tablespoons water**
      4 **cups (24 ounces) semisweet**
         chocolate chips, *divided*
      1 **teaspoon vanilla extract**
      2 **eggs**
    3/4 **cup all-purpose flour**
    1/2 **teaspoon salt**
    1/4 **teaspoon baking soda**
      2 **tablespoons shortening**
    1/2 **cup chopped pecans, toasted**

1. In a saucepan, bring sugar, butter and water to a boil over medium heat; remove from the heat. Stir in 1 cup of chocolate chips and vanilla; stir until smooth. Cool for 5 minutes.

2. Beat in eggs, one at a time, until well mixed. Combine flour, salt and baking soda; stir into chocolate mixture. Stir in another cup of chips.

3. Pour into a greased 9-in. square baking pan. Bake at 325° for 35 minutes. Cool completely.

Place in the freezer for 30-40 minutes (do not freeze completely). Cut into bars.

4. In a microwave or heavy saucepan, melt remaining chips with shortening; stir until smooth. Using a small fork, dip brownies to completely coat; shake off excess. Place on waxed paper-lined baking sheets; immediately sprinkle with nuts. Allow to set. Store in an airtight container in a cool place. **Yield:** 3 dozen.

Berries 'n' Cream Brownies —*Anna Lapp, New Holland, Pennsylvania*

      1 **package fudge brownie mix**
         (13-inch x 9-inch pan size)
      1 **carton (8 ounces) frozen whipped**
         topping, thawed
      4 **cups quartered fresh strawberries**
    1/3 **cup chocolate hard-shell ice cream**
         topping

1. Prepare and bake brownies according to package directions, using a greased 13-in. x 9-in. x 2-in. baking pan. Cool completely on a wire rack.

2. Spread whipped topping over brownies. Arrange strawberries cut side down over top. Drizzle with chocolate topping. Refrigerate for at least 30 minutes before serving. **Yield:** 12-15 servings.

Rich Chocolate Cream Bars –*Michele Paul, Fort Collins, Colorado*

1/2 cup butter
5 tablespoons baking cocoa
1/4 cup sugar
1 egg, beaten
1 teaspoon vanilla extract
1-1/2 cups graham cracker crumbs
(about 24 squares)
1 cup flaked coconut
1/2 cup chopped walnuts
FILLING:
1/4 cup butter, softened
3 tablespoons milk
2 tablespoons instant vanilla pudding
mix
2 cups confectioners' sugar
1 teaspoon vanilla extract
GLAZE:
4 squares (1 ounce *each*) semisweet
chocolate
1 tablespoon butter

1. In the top of a double boiler, combine butter, cocoa, sugar, egg and vanilla. Cook and stir over simmering water until mixture reaches 160° and is thickened. In a large bowl, combine graham cracker crumbs, coconut and walnuts. Stir in cocoa mixture; blend well. Press into a greased 9-in. square baking pan; set aside.

2. For filling, combine butter, milk and pudding mix in a mixing bowl. Gradually beat in confectioners' sugar and vanilla until smooth; spread over crust. For glaze, melt chocolate and butter; spread over filling. Cover and refrigerate until set. Cut into bars. **Yield:** about 3 dozen.

Peanut Butter Brownie Pizza –*Karen Jagger, Columbia City, Indiana*

1 package brownie mix (8-inch
square pan size)
1 package (8 ounces) cream cheese,
softened
1/3 cup peanut butter
1/4 cup sugar
3 large ripe bananas, cut into 1/4-inch
slices
1/2 cup orange *or* lemon juice
1/4 cup chopped peanuts
2 squares (1 ounce *each*) semisweet
chocolate
2 teaspoons butter

1. Prepare brownie batter according to package directions and spread into a greased 12-in. pizza pan. Bake at 375° for 15-20 minutes or until a toothpick inserted near the center comes out clean. Cool completely on a wire rack.

2. In a small mixing bowl, beat the cream cheese, peanut butter and sugar until smooth. Spread over crust. Toss bananas with juice; drain well. Arrange bananas over cream cheese mixture. Sprinkle with peanuts.

3. In a microwave, melt chocolate and butter. Drizzle over bananas. Refrigerate until chocolate is set. **Yield:** 12 servings.

Cookies & Confections

Chocolate Mint Candy —*Kendra Pedersen, Battle Ground, Washington*

2 **cups (12 ounces) semisweet chocolate chips**
1 **can (14 ounces) sweetened condensed milk,** *divided*
2 **teaspoons vanilla extract**
6 **ounces white candy coating**
2 **to 3 teaspoons peppermint extract**
3 **drops green food coloring**

1. In a heavy saucepan, melt chocolate chips with 1 cup milk. Remove from the heat; stir in vanilla. Spread half into a waxed paper-lined 8-in. square pan; chill for 10 minutes or until firm.

2. Meanwhile, in a heavy saucepan over low heat, cook and stir candy coating with remaining milk until coating is melted and mixture is smooth. Stir in peppermint extract and food coloring. Spread over bottom layer; chill for 10 minutes or until firm.

3. Warm remaining chocolate mixture if necessary; spread over mint layer. Chill for 2 hours or until firm. Remove from the pan; cut into 1-in. squares. **Yield:** about 2 pounds.

Butter Mints —*Bev Schloneger, Dalton, Ohio*

1/2 cup butter, softened
1 package (1 pound) confectioners' sugar
1 tablespoon half-and-half cream *or* milk
1 teaspoon vanilla extract
1/4 teaspoon peppermint extract
Red and green paste *or* liquid food coloring, optional

1. In a mixing bowl, cream the butter. Gradually add sugar, cream and extracts; beat on medium speed for 3-4 minutes. If desired, divide dough into portions and knead in food coloring.

2. Form into balls by teaspoonfuls; flatten into patties, or roll between two pieces of waxed paper to 1/8-in. thickness and cut into desired shapes. Cover and refrigerate for several hours or overnight. Store in the refrigerator. **Yield:** about 8 dozen.

Mountain Cookies —*Jeanne Adams, Richmond, Vermont*

1 cup butter, softened
1 cup confectioners' sugar
2 teaspoons vanilla extract
2 cups all-purpose flour
1/2 teaspoon salt
FILLING:
1 package (3 ounces) cream cheese, softened
1 cup confectioners' sugar
2 tablespoons all-purpose flour
1 teaspoon vanilla extract
1/2 cup finely chopped pecans
1/2 cup flaked coconut
TOPPING:
1/2 cup semisweet chocolate chips
2 tablespoons butter
2 tablespoons water
1/2 cup confectioners' sugar

1. In a mixing bowl, cream butter, sugar and vanilla. Combine flour and salt; gradually add to the creamed mixture and mix well. Shape into 1-in. balls; place 2 in. apart on ungreased baking sheets.

2. Make a deep indentation in the center of each cookie. Bake at 350° for 10-12 minutes or until the edges just start to brown. Remove to wire racks to cool completely.

3. For the filling, beat cream cheese, sugar, flour and vanilla in a mixing bowl. Add pecans and coconut; mix well. Spoon 1/2 teaspoon into each cookie. For topping, heat chocolate chips, butter and water in a small saucepan until melted. Stir in sugar. Drizzle over cookies. **Yield:** 4 dozen.

Candy Bar Fudge –*Lois Zigarac, Rochester Hills, Michigan*

1/2 cup butter
1/3 cup baking cocoa
1/4 cup packed brown sugar
1/4 cup milk
3-1/2 cups confectioners' sugar
1 teaspoon vanilla extract
30 caramels
1 tablespoon water
2 cups salted peanuts
1/2 cup semisweet chocolate chips
1/2 cup milk chocolate chips

1. In a microwave-safe bowl, combine the butter, cocoa, brown sugar and milk. Microwave on high until mixture boils, about 3 minutes. Stir in confectioners' sugar and vanilla. Pour into a greased 8-in. square baking pan.

2. In another microwave-safe bowl, heat caramels and water on high for 2 minutes or until melted. Stir in peanuts; spread over chocolate layer. Microwave chocolate chips on high for 1 minute or until melted; spread over caramel layer. Chill until firm. **Yield:** 2-3/4 pounds.

Editor's Note: This recipe was tested in a 700-watt microwave.

Meringue Kisses –*Tami Henke, Lockport, Illinois*

3 egg whites
1 teaspoon vanilla extract
1/4 teaspoon cream of tartar
Dash salt
1 cup sugar
Red and green food coloring, optional
44 chocolate kisses

1. In a mixing bowl, beat egg whites, vanilla, cream of tartar and salt, until soft peaks form. Gradually add sugar 2 tablespoons at a time, beating oh high until stiff peaks form, about 5-8 minutes. If desired, divide batter in half and fold in red and green food coloring.

2. Drop by rounded tablespoonfuls 1-1/2 in. apart onto lightly greased baking sheets. Press a chocolate kiss into the center of each cookie and cover it with meringue using a knife. Bake at 275° for 30-35 minutes or until firm to the touch. Immediately remove to a wire rack to cool. Store in an airtight container. **Yield:** 44 cookies.

Mint Sandwich Cookies —*Melissa Thompson, Anderson, Ohio*

1 can (16 ounces) vanilla frosting
1/2 teaspoon peppermint extract
3 to 5 drops green food coloring, optional
72 butter-flavored crackers
1 pound dark chocolate candy coating, coarsely chopped

1. In a bowl, combine the frosting, extract and food coloring if desired. Spread over half of the crackers; top with remaining crackers.

2. Place candy coating in a microwave-safe bowl. Microwave on high for 1-2 minutes or until smooth. Dip the cookies in coating. Place on waxed paper until chocolate is completely set. Store in an airtight container at room temperature. **Yield:** 3 dozen.

Coconut Macaroons —*Naomi Vining, Springdale, Arkansas*

1/2 cup egg whites (about 4)
1/4 teaspoon salt
1-1/4 cups sugar
1/2 teaspoon vanilla extract
3 cups flaked coconut

1. In a mixing bowl, beat egg whites and salt until soft peaks form. Gradually add sugar, beating until stiff peaks form, about 6 minutes. Beat in vanilla. Fold in coconut. Drop by rounded teaspoonfuls 2 in. apart onto lightly greased baking sheets.

2. Bake at 325° for 20 minutes or until firm to the touch. Remove to wire racks to cool. **Yield:** 5 dozen.

Honey Cream Taffy —*Iliene Taylor, Kearns, Utah*

1 tablespoon butter, softened
1 cup heavy whipping cream
2 cups honey
1 cup sugar

1. Grease a 15-in. x 10-in. x 1-in. baking pan with butter; place in the refrigerator. In a large deep heavy saucepan, combine cream and honey. Add sugar; cook over medium heat and stir with a wooden spoon until sugar is melted and mixture comes to a boil.

2. Cover pan with a tight-fitting lid and boil for 1 minute. Uncover; cook, without stirring, until a candy thermometer reaches 290° (soft-crack stage). Remove from the heat and pour into prepared pan (do not scrape sides of saucepan). Cool for 5 minutes. Using a wooden spoon, bring edges of honey mixture into center of pan. Cool 5-10 minutes longer or until cool enough to handle.

3. Using buttered hands, pull and stretch taffy until ridges form. (Taffy will lose its gloss and become light tan in color.) Pull into ropes about 1/2 in. thick. With a buttered kitchen scissors, cut into 1-in. pieces. Wrap individually in waxed paper. **Yield:** about 5 dozen.

Gifts from the Country Kitchen

Mint Sandwich Cookies

Marbled Orange Fudge —*Diane Wampler, Morristown, Tennessee*

1-1/2 teaspoons plus 3/4 cup butter, *divided*
   3 cups sugar
3/4 cup heavy whipping cream
   1 package (10 to 12 ounces) vanilla *or* white chips
   1 jar (7 ounces) marshmallow creme
   3 teaspoons orange extract
 12 drops yellow food coloring
   5 drops red food coloring

1. Grease a 13-in. x 9-in. x 2-in. pan with 1-1/2 teaspoons butter. In a heavy saucepan, combine the sugar, cream and remaining butter. Cook and stir over low heat until sugar is dissolved. Bring to a boil; cook and stir for 4 minutes. Remove from the heat; stir in chips and marshmallow creme until smooth.

2. Remove 1 cup and set aside. Add orange extract and food colorings to remaining mixture; stir until blended. Pour into prepared pan. Drop the reserved marshmallow mixture by tablespoonfuls over top; cut through mixture with a knife to swirl. Cover and refrigerate until set. Cut into squares. **Yield:** about 2-1/2 pounds.

Caramel Heavenlies —*Dawn Burns, Troy, Ohio*

 12 graham crackers (4-3/4 inches x 2-1/2 inches)
  2 cups miniature marshmallows
3/4 cup butter
3/4 cup packed brown sugar
  1 teaspoon ground cinnamon
  1 teaspoon vanilla extract
  1 cup sliced almonds
  1 cup flaked coconut

1. Line a 15-in. x 10-in. x 1-in. baking pan with foil. Place graham crackers in pan; cover with marshmallows. In a saucepan over medium heat, cook and stir butter, brown sugar and cinnamon until the butter is melted and sugar is dissolved. Remove from the heat; stir in vanilla. Spoon over the marshmallows. Sprinkle with almonds and coconut.

2. Bake at 350° for 14-16 minutes or until browned. Cool completely. Cut into 2-in. squares, then cut each square in half to form triangles. **Yield:** about 6 dozen.

Pulled Molasses Taffy —*Betty Woodman, Wolfe Island, Ontario*

5 teaspoons butter, softened, *divided*
1/4 cup water
1-1/4 cups packed brown sugar
2 tablespoons cider vinegar
1/4 teaspoon salt
1/3 cup molasses

1. Butter a 15-in. x 10-in. x 1-in. pan with 3 teaspoons butter; set aside. In a heavy saucepan, combine water, brown sugar, vinegar and salt. Bring to a boil over medium heat. Cook and stir until a candy thermometer reads 245° (firm-ball stage), stirring occasionally. Add molasses and remaining butter. Cook, uncovered, until a candy thermometer reads 260° (hard-ball stage), stirring occasionally.

2. Remove from the heat; pour into prepared pan. Cool for 5 minutes or until cool enough to handle. With buttered fingers, quickly pull half of the candy until firm but pliable. Pull and shape into a 1/2-in. rope. Cut into 1-1/4-in. pieces. Repeat with remaining taffy. Wrap pieces individually in foil or waxed paper; twist ends. Store in airtight containers in the refrigerator. Remove from the refrigerator 30 minutes before serving. **Yield:** 14-1/2 dozen.

Editor's Note: For easier candy making, enlist family members to help twist and pull the taffy with you. We recommend that you test your candy thermometer before each use by bringing water to a boil; the thermometer should read 212°. Adjust your recipe temperature up or down based on your test.

English Tea Cakes —*Beverly Christian, Fort Worth, Texas*

2 cups butter, softened
1 cup sugar
2 teaspoons vanilla extract
4 cups all-purpose flour
60 pecan halves

1. In a mixing bowl, cream butter and sugar. Beat in vanilla. Gradually add flour. Drop by heaping tablespoonfuls into greased muffin cups; flatten slightly. Press a pecan half in the center of each.

2. Bake at 350° for 10-12 minutes or until edges are lightly browned. Cool for 2 minutes in pans. Invert pans to remove. Place pecan side up on wire racks to cool completely. **Yield:** 5 dozen.

Double Delights —*Ruth Ann Stelfox, Raymond, Alberta*

CHOCOLATE DOUGH:
- 1 cup butter, softened
- 1-1/2 cups sugar
- 2 eggs
- 2 teaspoons vanilla extract
- 2 cups all-purpose flour
- 2/3 cup baking cocoa
- 3/4 teaspoon baking soda
- 1/2 teaspoon salt
- 1 cup coarsely chopped pecans
- 5 squares (1 ounce *each*) white baking chocolate, cut into chunks

VANILLA DOUGH:
- 1 cup butter, softened
- 1-1/2 cups sugar
- 2 eggs
- 2 teaspoons vanilla extract
- 2-3/4 cups all-purpose flour
- 2 teaspoons cream of tartar
- 1 teaspoon baking soda
- 1/2 teaspoon salt
- 1 cup coarsely chopped pecans
- 1 package (4 ounces) German sweet chocolate, cut into chunks

1. For chocolate dough, in a large mixing bowl, cream butter and sugar. Beat in eggs and vanilla. Combine the flour, cocoa, baking soda and salt; gradually add to creamed mixture. Stir in pecans and white chocolate.

2. For vanilla dough, in another large mixing bowl, cream butter and sugar. Beat in eggs and vanilla. Combine the flour, cream of tartar, baking soda and salt; gradually add to creamed mixture. Stir in pecans and German chocolate.

3. Cover and refrigerate both doughs for 2 hours. Divide both doughs in half. Shape each portion into a 12-in. roll; wrap in plastic wrap. Refrigerate for 3 hours or until firm.

4. Unwrap and cut each roll in half lengthwise. Place a chocolate half and vanilla half together, pressing to form a log; wrap in plastic wrap. Refrigerate for 1 hour or until the dough holds together when cut. Use a serrated knife to cut into 1/4-in. slices.

5. Place 2 in. apart on greased baking sheets. Bake at 350° for 8-10 minutes or until set. Remove to wire racks to cool. **Yield:** about 15 dozen.

Double Butterscotch Cookies —*Beverly Duncan, Big Prairie, Ohio*

1/2 cup butter, softened
1/2 cup shortening
  4 cups packed brown sugar
  4 eggs
  1 tablespoon vanilla extract
  6 cups all-purpose flour
  1 tablespoon baking soda
  1 tablespoon cream of tartar
  1 teaspoon salt
  1 package English toffee bits
      (10 ounces) *or* almond brickle chips
      (7-1/2 ounces)
  1 cup finely chopped pecans

1. In a mixing bowl, cream the butter, shortening and brown sugar until light and fluffy. Add eggs, one at a time, beating well after each addition. Beat in vanilla. Combine flour, baking soda, cream of tartar and salt; gradually add to the creamed mixture and mix well. Stir in toffee bits and pecans. Shape into three 14-in. rolls; wrap each in plastic wrap. Refrigerate for 4 hours or until firm.

2. Unwrap and cut into 1/2-in. slices. Place 2 in. apart on greased baking sheets. Bake at 375° for 9-11 minutes or until lightly browned. Cool for 1-2 minutes before removing to wire racks to cool completely. **Yield:** about 7 dozen.

Creamy Caramels —*Marcie Wolfe, Williamsburg, Virginia*

  1 cup sugar
  1 cup dark corn syrup
  1 cup butter
  1 can (14 ounces) sweetened
      condensed milk
  1 teaspoon vanilla extract

1. Line an 8-in. square pan with foil and butter the foil; set aside. Combine sugar, corn syrup and butter in a 3-qt. saucepan. Bring to a boil over medium heat, stirring constantly. Boil slowly for 4 minutes without stirring.

2. Remove from the heat and stir in milk. Reduce heat to medium-low and cook until candy thermometer reads 238° (soft-ball stage), stirring constantly. Remove from the heat and stir in vanilla.

3. Pour into prepared pan. Cool. Remove from pan and cut into 1-in. squares. Wrap individually in waxed paper; twist ends. **Yield:** 64 pieces.

Editor's Note: We recommend that you test your candy thermometer before each use. Bring water to a boil; the thermometer should read 212°. Adjust your recipe temperature up or down based on your test.

English Toffee –*Don McVay, Wilsonville, Oregon*

1 tablespoon plus 2 cups butter,
   softened, *divided*
2 cups sugar
1 tablespoon light corn syrup
1/4 teaspoon salt
1 cup milk chocolate chips
1 cup chopped pecans

1. Grease a 15-in. x 10-in. x 1-in. baking pan with 1 tablespoon butter; set aside. In a heavy 3-qt. saucepan, melt the remaining butter. Add sugar, corn syrup and salt; cook and stir over medium heat until a candy thermometer reads 295° (hard-crack stage). Quickly pour into prepared pan. Let stand at room temperature until cool, about 1 hour.

2. In a microwave, melt chocolate chips; spread over toffee. Sprinkle with pecans. Let stand for 1 hour. Break into bite-size pieces. Store in an airtight container at room temperature. **Yield:** about 2 pounds.

  Editor's Note: We recommend that you test your candy thermometer before each use by bringing water to a boil; the thermometer should read 212°. Adjust your recipe temperature up or down based on your test.

Fudge-Topped Orange Cookies –*Lisa Evans, Rileyville, Virginia*

3/4 cup butter, softened
1 cup sugar
1 egg
2 egg yolks
2 teaspoons grated orange peel
1-1/2 teaspoons orange extract
2 cups all-purpose flour
1 teaspoon ground ginger
1/2 teaspoon baking soda
TOPPING:
1 jar (7 ounces) marshmallow creme
3/4 cup sugar
1/3 cup evaporated milk
2 tablespoons butter
1/8 teaspoon salt
1 cup (6 ounces) semisweet chocolate
   chips
1/2 teaspoon vanilla extract

1. In a mixing bowl, cream butter and sugar. Beat in the egg, egg yolks, orange peel and extract. Combine the flour, ginger and baking soda; gradually add to creamed mixture.

2. Drop by rounded tablespoonfuls 2 in. apart onto ungreased baking sheets. Bake at 300° for 21-23 minutes or until golden brown. Remove to wire racks to cool.

3. In a saucepan, combine the marshmallow creme, sugar, milk, butter and salt. Bring to a rolling boil over medium heat; boil for 5 minutes, stirring constantly. Remove from the heat. Add chocolate chips and vanilla; stir until chips are melted. Spread over tops of cookies. **Yield:** 2 dozen.

English Toffee

Orange Chocolate Meltaways –*Lori Kostecki, Wausau, Wisconsin*

1 package (11-1/2 ounces) milk chocolate chips
1 cup (6 ounces) semisweet chocolate chips
3/4 cup heavy whipping cream
1 teaspoon grated orange peel
2-1/2 teaspoons orange extract
1-1/2 cups finely chopped toasted pecans
COATING:
1 cup (6 ounces) milk chocolate chips
2 tablespoons shortening

1. Place chocolate chips in a mixing bowl; set aside. In a saucepan, bring cream and orange peel to a gentle boil; immediately pour over chips. Let stand for 1 minute; whisk until smooth. Add the extract. Cover and chill for 35 minutes or until mixture begins to thicken.

2. Beat for 10-15 seconds or just until mixture lightens in color (do not overbeat). Spoon rounded teaspoonfuls onto waxed paper-lined baking sheets. Cover and chill for 5 minutes. Gently shape into balls; roll half in pecans.

3. In a microwave or heavy saucepan, melt chocolate and shortening; stir until smooth. Dip remaining balls in chocolate. Place on waxed paper to set. Store in the refrigerator. **Yield:** 6 dozen.

Fancy Peanut Butter Cookies –*Janet Hooper, Emporium, Pennsylvania*

1 cup shortening
1 cup peanut butter
1 cup sugar
1 cup packed brown sugar
2 eggs
1/4 cup milk
2 teaspoons vanilla extract
3-1/2 cups all-purpose flour
2 teaspoons baking soda
1 teaspoon salt
FROSTING:
1/4 cup butter, softened
1/4 cup shortening
1/4 cup peanut butter
4 cups confectioners' sugar
1/4 cup milk
1 teaspoon vanilla extract
Dash salt
ICING:
1/2 cup semisweet chocolate chips, melted
2 tablespoons milk

1. In a mixing bowl, cream shortening, peanut butter and sugars. Add eggs, one at a time, beating well after each addition. Beat in milk and vanilla. Combine flour, baking soda and salt; gradually add to the creamed mixture.

2. Roll into 1-in. balls. Place 2 in. apart on ungreased baking sheets. Bake at 375° for 10-12 minutes or until golden brown. Remove to wire racks.

3. For frosting, cream butter, shortening, peanut butter and confectioners' sugar in a mixing bowl. Beat in milk, vanilla and salt until smooth. Frost cooled cookies. Combine icing ingredients; drizzle over frosting. **Yield:** 7-1/2 dozen.

Perfect Peppermint Patties –*Joanne Adams, Bath, Maine*

3-3/4 cups confectioners' sugar
   3 tablespoons butter, softened
   2 to 3 teaspoons peppermint extract
1/2 teaspoon vanilla extract
1/4 cup evaporated milk
   2 cups (12 ounces) semisweet chocolate chips
   2 tablespoons shortening

1. In a bowl, combine first four ingredients. Add milk and mix well. Roll into 1-in. balls and place on a waxed paper-lined baking sheet. Flatten with a glass to 1/4 in. Cover and freeze for 30 minutes.

2. In a microwave or heavy saucepan, melt chocolate chips and shortening; stir until smooth. Dip patties; place on waxed paper to set. **Yield:** about 5 dozen.

Surprise Meringues –*Gloria Grant, Sterling, Illinois*

   3 egg whites
   1 teaspoon vanilla extract
1/8 teaspoon cream of tartar
1/8 teaspoon salt
3/4 cup sugar
   1 cup (6 ounces) miniature semisweet chocolate chips
1/4 cup chopped pecans *or* walnuts

1. In a mixing bowl, beat egg whites, vanilla, cream of tartar and salt on medium speed until soft peaks form. Gradually add sugar, 2 tablespoons at a time, beating on high until stiff peaks form and sugar is dissolved, about 6 minutes. Fold in the chocolate chips and nuts.

2. Drop by rounded teaspoonfuls 2 in. apart onto parchment paper-lined baking sheets. Bake at 250° for 40-45 minutes or until firm to the touch. Turn oven off; leave meringues in oven for 1-1/2 hours. Remove to wire racks. Store in an airtight container. **Yield:** 4 dozen.

Cherry Cheese Windmills —*Helen McGibbon, Downers Grove, Illinois*

1/3 cup butter, softened
1/3 cup shortening
3/4 cup sugar
1 egg
1 tablespoon milk
1 teaspoon vanilla extract
2 cups all-purpose flour
1-1/2 teaspoons baking powder
1/4 teaspoon salt

FILLING:
1 package (3 ounces) cream cheese, softened
1/4 cup sugar
1/4 teaspoon almond extract
1/2 cup finely chopped maraschino cherries
1/4 cup sliced almonds, toasted and chopped

1. In a large mixing bowl, cream the butter, shortening and sugar. Beat in the egg, milk and vanilla. Combine flour, baking powder and salt; gradually add to creamed mixture. Divide dough in half. Cover and refrigerate for 3 hours or until easy to handle.

2. In a small mixing bowl, beat cream cheese, sugar and extract. Fold in cherries. On a floured surface, roll each portion of dough into a 10-in. square. With a sharp knife or pastry wheel, cut into 2-1/2-in. squares. Place 2 in. apart on ungreased baking sheets. Make 1-in. cuts from each corner toward the center of the dough.

3. Drop teaspoonfuls of filling in the center of each square; sprinkle with almonds. Fold alternating points to the center to form a windmill; moisten points with water and pinch gently at center to seal. Bake at 350° for 8-10 minutes or until set. Cool on wire racks. **Yield:** about 2-1/2 dozen.

Three-Chocolate Fudge — *Betty Grantham, Hanceville, Alabama*

3-1/3 cups sugar
   1 cup butter
   1 cup packed dark brown sugar
   1 can (12 ounces) evaporated milk
 32 large marshmallows, halved
   2 cups (12 ounces) semisweet chocolate
      chips
   2 milk chocolate candy bars (7 ounces
      each), broken
   2 squares (1 ounce *each*) semisweet
      baking chocolate, chopped
   1 teaspoon vanilla extract
   2 cups chopped pecans

1. In a large saucepan, combine first four ingredients. Cook and stir over medium heat until sugar is dissolved. Bring to a rapid boil; boil for 5 minutes, stirring constantly.

2. Remove from the heat; stir in marshmallows until melted. Stir in chocolate chips until melted. Add chocolate bars and baking chocolate; stir until melted. Fold in vanilla and pecans; mix well.

3. Pour into a greased 15-in. x 10-in. x 1-in. baking pan. Chill until firm. Cut into squares. **Yield:** 5-1/2 pounds.

Toasted Coconut Truffles — *Beth Nagel, West Lafayette, Indiana*

   4 cups (24 ounces) semisweet chocolate
      chips
   1 package (8 ounces) cream cheese,
      softened and cubed
3/4 cup sweetened condensed milk
   3 teaspoons vanilla extract
   2 teaspoons water
   1 pound white candy coating
   2 tablespoons flaked coconut, finely
      chopped and toasted

1. In a microwave or heavy saucepan, melt chocolate chips; stir until smooth. Add the cream cheese, milk, vanilla and water; beat with a hand mixer until blended. Cover and refrigerate until easy to handle, about 1-1/2 hours.

2. Shape into 1-in. balls and place on waxed paper-lined baking sheets. Loosely cover and refrigerate for 1-2 hours or until firm.

3. In a microwave or heavy saucepan, melt candy coating, stirring often. Dip balls in coating; place on waxed paper-lined baking sheets. Sprinkle with coconut. Refrigerate until firm, about 15 minutes. Store in the refrigerator in an airtight container. **Yield:** about 5-1/2 dozen.

Cranberry Macadamia Bark –*Pamela Galiardi, San Jose, California*

1 pound white candy coating, cut into
  pieces
1 jar (3-1/2 ounces) macadamia nuts
1/2 cup dried cranberries

Melt coating in a saucepan over medium-low heat, stirring until smooth. Add nuts and cranberries; mix well. Spread onto a foil-lined baking sheet. Cool. Break into pieces. **Yield:** 1-1/4 pounds.

Peanut Butter Fudge –*Eleanore Peterson, Fort Atkinson, Wisconsin*

1 pound white candy coating, cut
  into pieces
1 cup creamy peanut butter
1 cup coarsely chopped walnuts

Melt coating in a saucepan over medium-low heat, stirring constantly until smooth. Remove from the heat; stir in peanut butter and walnuts. Spread into a greased 8-in. square pan. Chill until firm. Cut into squares. **Yield:** 1-3/4 pounds.

Goody-Goody Gumdrops –*Sue Ann Bunt, Painted Post, New York*

3 envelopes unflavored gelatin
1-1/4 cups water, *divided*
1-1/2 cups sugar
1/4 to 1/2 teaspoon peppermint extract
Green and red food coloring
Additional sugar

1. In a small bowl, sprinkle gelatin over 1/2 cup water; let stand for 5 minutes. In a saucepan, bring sugar and remaining water to a boil over medium heat, stirring constantly. Add the gelatin; reduce heat. Simmer and stir for 5 minutes. Remove from the heat and stir in extract.

2. Divide mixture into two bowls; add four drops green food coloring to one bowl and four drops red to the other. Pour into two greased 8-in. x 4-in. x 2-in. loaf pans. Chill 3 hours or until firm.

3. Loosen edges from pan with a knife; turn onto a sugared board. Cut into 1/2-in. cubes; roll in sugar. Let stand at room temperature, uncovered, for 3-4 hours, turning every hour so all sides dry. Cover and chill. **Yield:** about 1 pound.

Easy Chocolate Drops –*Heather De Cal, Terrace Bay, Ontario*

1 cup (6 ounces) semisweet chocolate
  chips
1 cup (6 ounces) butterscotch chips
1 cup shoestring potato sticks
1 cup salted peanuts

1. In a 2-qt. microwave-safe bowl, heat chips on high for 2 minutes or until melted, stirring once. Stir in potato sticks and peanuts.

2. Drop by teaspoonfuls onto waxed paper-lined baking sheets. Chill until set, about 15 minutes. Store in airtight containers. **Yield:** 3-1/2 dozen.

Editor's Note: This recipe was tested in a 700-watt microwave.

Clockwise from top: Cranberry
Macadamia Bark, Goody-Goody
Gumdrops, Easy Chocolate
Drops and Peanut Butter Fudge

Dipped Gingersnaps –*Laura Kimball, West Jordan, Utah*

2 cups sugar
1-1/2 cups vegetable oil
2 eggs
1/2 cup molasses
4 cups all-purpose flour
4 teaspoons baking soda
1 tablespoon ground ginger
2 teaspoons ground cinnamon
1 teaspoon salt
Additional sugar
2 packages (10 to12 ounces *each*)
vanilla or white chips
1/4 cup shortening

1. In a mixing bowl, combine sugar and oil; mix well. Add eggs, one at a time, beating well after each addition. Stir in molasses. Combine dry ingredients; gradually add to creamed mixture and mix well.

2. Shape into 3/4-in. balls and roll in sugar. Place 2 in. apart on ungreased baking sheets. Bake at 350° for 10-12 minutes or until cookie springs back when touched lightly. Remove to wire racks to cool.

3. Melt chips with shortening in a small saucepan over low heat. Dip the cookies halfway; shake off excess. Place on waxed paper-lined baking sheets to set. **Yield:** about 14-1/2 dozen.

Molasses Raisin Chews –*Barbara Parker, Middlefield, Connecticut*

1/2 cup shortening
1 cup sugar
1 cup molasses
4 cups all-purpose flour
2 teaspoons baking soda
2 teaspoons ground cinnamon
1 teaspoon ground cloves
1/4 teaspoon salt
1 cup milk
1 cup raisins

1. In a mixing bowl, cream shortening and sugar. Beat in molasses. Combine flour, baking soda, cinnamon, cloves and salt; add to the creamed mixture alternately with milk.

2. Drop by heaping tablespoonfuls 2 in. apart onto greased baking sheets. Arrange three raisins on each cookie. Bake at 350° for 10-12 minutes or until set. Remove to wire racks to cool. **Yield:** about 5-1/2 dozen.

Surprise Package Cookies —Lorraine Meyer, Bend, Oregon

1 cup butter, softened
1 cup sugar
1/2 cup packed brown sugar
2 eggs
1 teaspoon vanilla extract
3 cups all-purpose flour
1 teaspoon baking powder
1/2 teaspoon salt
65 mint Andes candies

1. In a mixing bowl, cream butter and sugars. Add eggs, one at a time, beating well after each addition. Beat in vanilla. Combine the flour, baking powder and salt; gradually add to creamed mixture. Cover and refrigerate for 2 hours or until easy to handle. With floured hands, shape a tablespoonful of dough around 42 candies, forming rectangular cookies.

2. Place 2 in. apart on greased baking sheets. Bake at 375° for 10-12 minutes or until edges are golden brown. Remove to wire racks to cool. In a microwave or saucepan, melt the remaining candies; stir until smooth. Drizzle over cookies. **Yield:** 3-1/2 dozen.

Orange Taffy —Christine Olson, Horse Creek, California

2 cups sugar
2 cups light corn syrup
1 can (6 ounces) frozen orange juice
   concentrate, undiluted
Dash salt
1 cup half-and-half cream
1/2 cup butter

1. In a heavy saucepan, combine first four ingredients. Cook and stir over medium heat until sugar is dissolved. Bring to a rapid boil and cook until a candy thermometer reads 245° (firm-ball stage).

2. Add cream and butter; heat and stir until mixture reaches 245° again.

3. Pour into a greased 15-in. x 10-in. x 1-in. pan; cool. When cool enough to handle, roll into 1-1/2-in. logs or 1-in. balls. Wrap each in foil or waxed paper; twist ends. **Yield:** about 6 dozen.

Editor's Note: We recommend that you test your candy thermometer before each use by bringing water to a boil; the thermometer should read 212°. Adjust your recipe temperature up or down based on your test.

Mocha Truffles –*Stacy Abell, Olathe, Kansas*

2 packages (12 ounces each) semisweet
   chocolate chips
1 package (8 ounces) cream cheese,
   softened
3 tablespoons instant coffee granules
2 teaspoons water
1 pound dark chocolate candy coating
White candy coating, optional

1. In a microwave-safe bowl or heavy saucepan, melt chocolate chips. Add cream cheese, coffee and water; mix well. Chill until firm enough to shape.

2. Shape into 1-in. balls and place on a waxed paper-lined baking sheet. Chill for 1-2 hours or until firm.

3. Melt chocolate coating in microwave-safe bowl or heavy saucepan. Dip balls and place on waxed paper to set. If desired, melt white coating and drizzle over truffles. **Yield:** about 5-1/2 dozen.

   Editor's Note: Truffles can be frozen for several months before dipping in chocolate. Thaw in the refrigerator before dipping.

Viennese Fudge –*Loranne Weir, San Ramon, California*

1 teaspoon plus 3 tablespoons butter,
   divided
2 cups sugar
1 cup evaporated milk
1/2 teaspoon salt
1 cup miniature marshmallows
1-1/2 cups semisweet chocolate chips
2 teaspoons vanilla extract
1-1/2 cups ground hazelnuts, toasted

1. Line an 8-in. square pan with foil and butter the foil with 1 teaspoon butter; set aside. In a large saucepan, combine the sugar, milk, salt and remaining butter. Bring to a boil over medium heat, stirring constantly. Boil and stir for 6 minutes.

2. Remove from the heat; stir in marshmallows until melted. Add chocolate chips and stir until melted. Stir in vanilla and nuts. Pour into prepared pan. Let stand at room temperature until cool.

3. Using foil, lift fudge out of pan; cut into 1-in. squares. Store in an airtight container in the refrigerator. **Yield:** 2 pounds.

Hard Candy Peppermint Twists —Sue Jent, Golcolda, Illinois

1 cup water
1 tablespoon white vinegar
2 cups sugar
1-1/2 teaspoons peppermint extract
1/8 teaspoon red food coloring

1. Coat two 9-in. square baking pans with nonstick cooking spray; set aside. (Do not use butter or foil to prepare pans.)

2. In a heavy saucepan, combine water and vinegar. Add sugar. Cook and stir over medium heat until sugar is dissolved and mixture comes to a boil, about 8 minutes. (If sugar crystals are present, cover saucepan for 1-1/2 to 2 minutes to allow steam to wash crystals down.) Cook, without stirring, until a candy thermometer reads 300° (hard-crack stage), about 26 minutes.

3. Combine peppermint extract and food coloring. Remove syrup from the heat; stir in peppermint mixture until well blended (mixture will bubble up slightly). Keep face away from mixture as odor is strong. Immediately and carefully pour into prepared pans (do not scrape saucepan or tilt pans to spread mixture evenly). Cool for 1-1/2 to 2 minutes.

4. Using a sharp knife, score candy into 1/2-in.- to 3/4-in.- wide pieces, about 3 in. long. Place both pans in a warm oven (150° or your oven's lowest temperature) for about 5 minutes or until candy is warm enough to cut but cool enough to handle.

5. Using a heavy-duty kitchen scissors, cut along scored lines, one piece at a time. Immediately

wrap each piece around the handle of a wooden spoon; remove candy and place on waxed paper to harden. Continue cutting and wrapping until mixture in pan begins to harden. Return pan to oven for at least 5 minutes. Meanwhile, remove second pan from the oven. Cut and wrap as before until mixture begins to harden. Return to oven and repeat with the first pan. Repeat until all mixture is cut and formed into twists. **Yield:** about 1/2 pound.

Editor's Note: We recommend that you test your candy thermometer before each use by bringing water to a boil; the thermometer should read 212°. Adjust your recipe temperature up or down based on your test.

Coconut Bonbons —Beverly Cray, Epping, New Hampshire

1/2 cup butter, softened
2 pounds confectioners' sugar
1 can (14 ounces) sweetened condensed milk
4 cups chopped pecans
1 package (10 ounces) flaked coconut
1 teaspoon vanilla extract
2 cups (12 ounces) semisweet chocolate chips
1 tablespoon shortening

1. In a mixing bowl, cream butter and sugar. Add the milk, pecans, coconut and vanilla; mix well. Shape into 1-in. balls. Refrigerate for 30-45 minutes or until firm.

2. In a microwave or heavy saucepan, melt the chips and shortening; stir until smooth. Dip balls and place on waxed paper to set. Store in an airtight container at room temperature. **Yield:** about 21 dozen.

Editor's Note: Candies can be frozen for up to 3 months before dipping in chocolate. Thaw in refrigerator before dipping.

Fruity Pastel Cookies —*Conna Duff, Lexington, Virginia*

3/4 cup butter, softened
1/2 cup sugar
1 package (3 ounces) lime gelatin *or* flavor of your choice
1 egg
1/2 teaspoon vanilla extract
1-3/4 cups all-purpose flour
1/2 teaspoon baking powder
Red and green colored sugar *and/or* sprinkles

1. In a mixing bowl, cream butter, sugar and gelatin powder. Beat in egg and vanilla. Combine flour and baking powder; gradually add to creamed mixture and mix well.

2. Using a cookie press fitted with the disk of your choice, press dough 2 in. apart onto ungreased baking sheets. Decorate as desired with colored sugar and/or sprinkles. Bake at 400° for 6-8 minutes or until set (do not brown). Remove to wire racks to cool. Decorate as desired. **Yield:** 6 dozen.

Raspberry Ribbons —*Patsy Wolfenden, Golden, British Columbia*

1 cup butter, softened
1/2 cup sugar
1 egg
1 teaspoon vanilla extract
2-1/4 cups all-purpose flour
1/2 teaspoon baking powder
1/4 teaspoon salt
1/2 cup raspberry jam
GLAZE:
1 cup confectioners' sugar
2 tablespoons evaporated milk
1/2 teaspoon vanilla extract

1. In a mixing bowl, cream butter and sugar. Beat in egg and vanilla. Combine the flour, baking powder and salt; gradually add to creamed mixture and mix well. Divide dough into four portions; shape each into a 10-in. x 2-1/2-in. log. Place 4 in. apart on greased or foil-lined baking sheets.

2. Make a 1/2-in. depression down the center of each log. Bake at 350° for 10 minutes. Fill depressions with jam. Bake 10-15 minutes longer or until lightly browned. Cool for 2 minutes. Remove to a cutting board; cut into 3/4-in. slices. Place on wire racks.

3. In a small bowl, combine glaze ingredients until smooth. Drizzle over warm cookies. Cool completely. **Yield:** about 5 dozen.

Top to Bottom: Fruity Pastel
Cookies and Raspberry Ribbons

Cranberry Chip Cookies —*Jo Ann McCarthy, Canton, Massachuetts*

1/2 **cup butter, softened**
1/2 **cup shortening**
3/4 **cup sugar**
3/4 **cup packed brown sugar**
  2 **eggs**
  1 **teaspoon vanilla extract**
2-1/4 **cups all-purpose flour**
  1 **teaspoon baking soda**
1/2 **teaspoon salt**
  1 **cup semisweet chocolate chips**
  1 **cup vanilla *or* white chips**
  1 **cup dried cranberries**
  1 **cup chopped pecans**

1. In a mixing bowl, cream butter, shortening and sugars. Add eggs, one at a time, beating well after each addition. Beat in vanilla. Combine flour, baking soda and salt; gradually add to the creamed mixture. Stir in the chips, cranberries and pecans.

2. Drop by tablespoonfuls 2 in. apart onto ungreased baking sheets. Bake at 375° for 9-11 minutes or until golden brown. Cool for 2 minutes before removing to wire racks to cool completely. **Yield:** 9 dozen.

Chocolate Mint Wafers —*Annette Esay, Durham, Ontario*

2/3 **cup butter, softened**
1/2 **cup sugar**
1/2 **cup packed brown sugar**
1/4 **cup milk**
  1 **egg**
  2 **cups all-purpose flour**
3/4 **cup baking cocoa**
  1 **teaspoon baking powder**
1/2 **teaspoon baking soda**
1/4 **teaspoon salt**
FILLING:
2-3/4 **cups confectioners' sugar**
1/4 **cup half-and-half cream**
1/4 **teaspoon peppermint extract**
1/4 **teaspoon salt**
Green food coloring

1. In a mixing bowl, cream butter and sugars. Add milk and egg; mix well. Combine dry ingredients; gradually add to creamed mixture and mix well. Cover and chill 2 hours or until firm.

2. Roll chilled dough on a floured surface to 1/8-in. thickness. Cut with a 1-1/2-in. cookie cutter. Place 1 in. apart on greased baking sheets. Bake at 375° for 5-6 minutes or until edges are lightly browned. Remove to wire racks to cool completely.

3. Combine filling ingredients; spread on half of the cookies and top with another cookie. **Yield:** about 7-1/2 dozen.

Chocolate Pecan Caramels –*June Humphrey, Strongsville, Ohio*

1 tablespoon plus 1 cup butter (no substitutes), softened, *divided*
1-1/2 cups coarsely chopped pecans, toasted
1 cup (6 ounces) semisweet chocolate chips
2 cups packed brown sugar
1 cup light corn syrup
1/4 cup water
1 can (14 ounces) sweetened condensed milk
2 teaspoons vanilla extract

1. Line a 13-in. x 9-in. x 2-in. baking pan with foil; butter the foil with 1 tablespoon butter. Sprinkle with pecans and chocolate chips; set aside.

2. In a heavy saucepan over medium heat, melt remaining butter. Add brown sugar, corn syrup and water. Cook and stir until mixture comes to a boil. Stir in milk. Cook, stirring constantly, until a candy thermometer reads 248° (firm-ball stage). Remove from the heat and stir in vanilla.

Pour into prepared pan (do not scrape saucepan). Cool completely before cutting. **Yield:** about 2-1/2 pounds (about 6-3/4 dozen).

Editor's Note: We recommend that you test your candy thermometer before each use by bringing water to a boil; the thermometer should read 212°. Adjust your recipe temperature up or down based on your test.

Maple Peanut Delights –*Katie Stutzman, Goshen, Indiana*

1 package (8 ounces) cream cheese, softened
1/2 cup butter, softened
6 cups confectioners' sugar
1 teaspoon maple flavoring
2 pounds dark chocolate candy coating
1 cup chopped peanuts

1. In a mixing bowl, beat cream cheese, butter, confectioners' sugar and flavoring until smooth. Cover and refrigerate for 1 hour.

2. Shape into 1-in. balls. In a microwave or heavy saucepan, melt candy coating, stirring often. Dip balls in coating; sprinkle with peanuts. Place on waxed paper-lined baking sheets until set. Store in the refrigerator. **Yield:** about 8 dozen.

Chocolate Truffle Cookies —*Delaine Fortenberry, McComb, Mississippi*

4 squares (1 ounce *each*) unsweetened chocolate
2 cups (12 ounces) semisweet chocolate chips, *divided*
1/3 cup butter
1 cup sugar
3 eggs
1-1/2 teaspoons vanilla extract
1/2 cup all-purpose flour
2 tablespoons baking cocoa
1/4 teaspoon baking powder
1/4 teaspoon salt
Confectioners' sugar

1. In a microwave or heavy saucepan, melt unsweetened chocolate, 1 cup of chocolate chips and butter; stir until smooth. Cool for 10 minutes.

2. In a mixing bowl, beat sugar and eggs for 2 minutes. Beat in vanilla and the chocolate mixture. Combine flour, cocoa, baking powder and salt; beat into chocolate mixture. Stir in remaining chocolate chips. Cover and refrigerate for at least 3 hours.

3. Remove about 1 cup of dough. With lightly floured hands, roll into 1-in. balls. Place on ungreased baking sheets. Bake at 350° for 10-12 minutes or until lightly puffed and set. Cool on pan 3-4 minutes before removing to a wire rack to cool completely. Repeat with remaining dough. Dust with confectioners' sugar. **Yield:** about 4 dozen.

Cashew Crickle —*Katly Kittell, Lenexa, Kansas*

2 cups sugar
2/3 cup corn syrup
1/2 cup water
3 tablespoons butter
1 teaspoon vanilla extract
1/2 teaspoon baking soda
2 cups salted cashews

1. In a large saucepan, combine sugar, corn syrup and water; bring to a boil, stirring constantly, until sugar is dissolved. Cook, without stirring, over medium heat until a candy thermometer reads 300° (hard-crack stage).

2. Remove from the heat; stir in butter, vanilla and baking soda. Add cashews. Pour into a greased 15-in. x 10-in. x 1-in. baking pan. Cool; break into pieces. **Yield:** about 2 pounds.

Editor's Note: We recommend that you test your candy thermometer before each use by bringing water to a boil; the thermometer should read 212°. Adjust your recipe temperature up or down based on your test.

Breads & Rolls

Apricot Mini Loaves —*Kelly Koutahi, Moore, Oklahoma*

1 egg, lightly beaten
6 tablespoons milk
5 tablespoons butter, melted
4-1/2 teaspoons honey
1/2 teaspoon vanilla extract
1 cup pancake mix
1/4 cup finely chopped walnuts
1/4 cup finely chopped dried apricots
2 tablespoons raisins
GLAZE:
1/2 cup confectioners' sugar
1 teaspoon honey
1/8 teaspoon ground cloves
2 to 3 teaspoons milk

1. In a bowl, combine the egg, milk, butter, honey and vanilla; stir in the pancake mix just until moistened. Fold in the walnuts, apricots and raisins. Pour into two greased 4-1/2-in. x 2-1/2-in. x 1-1/2-in. loaf pans.

2. Bake at 350° for 22-28 minutes or until a toothpick inserted near the center comes out clean. Cool for 5 minutes before removing from pans to wire racks.

3. In a small bowl, combine the glaze ingredients. Drizzle over warm loaves. Cool. **Yield:** 2 loaves.

Chocolate Pinwheel Bread —Dawn Onuffer, Freeport, Florida

1 package (1/4 ounce) active dry yeast
1 cup warm milk (110° to 115°)
1/4 cup sugar
1 teaspoon salt
2 eggs
4 ounces cream cheese, softened
4 to 4-1/2 cups bread flour

FILLING:
4 ounces cream cheese, softened
1/2 cup confectioners' sugar
2 tablespoons baking cocoa
1 cup (6 ounces) semisweet chocolate chips
1 egg, beaten

1. In a large mixing bowl, dissolve yeast in milk. Add sugar, salt, eggs, cream cheese and 2 cups flour; beat until smooth. Stir in enough remaining flour to form a soft dough. Turn onto a floured surface; knead until smooth and elastic, about 6-8 minutes. Place in a greased bowl, turning once to grease top. Cover and let rise in a warm place until doubled, about 1 hour.

2. Punch dough down. Turn onto a floured surface; divide in half. Roll each portion into a 12-in. x 8-in. rectangle. In a mixing bowl, beat cream cheese, confectioners' sugar and cocoa until smooth. Spread over each rectangle to within 1/2 in. of edges. Sprinkle with chocolate chips. Roll up jelly-roll style, starting with a short side; pinch seam to seal. Place seam side down in two greased 9-in. x 5-in. x 3-in. loaf pans. Cover and let rise until doubled, about 45 minutes.

3. Brush tops of loaves with egg. Bake at 350° for 25 minutes. Cover loosely with foil. Bake 15-20 minutes longer or until loaves sound hollow when tapped. Remove from pans to wire racks to cool. **Yield:** 2 loaves.

Coconut Pumpkin Loaves —Anne Smithson, Cary, North Carolina

5 eggs
2 cups canned pumpkin
2 cups sugar
1-1/4 cups vegetable oil
3 cups all-purpose flour
2 packages (3.4 ounces *each*) instant coconut pudding mix
3 teaspoons ground cinnamon
2 teaspoons baking soda
1 teaspoon ground nutmeg
3/4 cup chopped pecans

1. In a large mixing bowl, beat the eggs and pumpkin until smooth. Add sugar and oil; mix well. Combine the flour, pudding mixes, cinnamon, baking soda and nutmeg; add to the pumpkin mixture. Stir in nuts.

2. Transfer to three greased and floured 8-in. x 4-in. x 2-in. loaf pans. Bake at 350° for 60-65 minutes or until a toothpick inserted near the center comes out clean. Cool for 10 minutes before removing from pans to wire racks to cool completely. **Yield:** 3 loaves.

Cranberry Fruit Bread — *Ellen Puotinen, Tower, Minnesota*

1 package (12 ounces) fresh *or* frozen
    cranberries, halved
2 cups pecan halves
1 cup chopped mixed candied fruit
1 cup chopped dates
1 cup golden raisins
1 tablespoon grated orange peel
4 cups all-purpose flour, *divided*
2 cups sugar
1 tablespoon baking powder
1 teaspoon baking soda
1/4 teaspoon salt
2 eggs
1 cup orange juice
1/4 cup vegetable oil
1/4 cup warm water

1. Combine the cranberries, pecans, fruit, dates, raisins and orange peel with 1/4 cup flour; set aside. In another bowl, combine sugar, baking powder, baking soda, salt and remaining flour; set aside.

2. In a large mixing bowl, beat eggs. Add orange juice, oil and water. Add flour mixture; stir just until combined. Fold in cranberry mixture.

3. Spoon into three greased and waxed paper-lined 8-in. x 4-in. x 2-in. loaf pans. Bake at 350° for 60-65 minutes or until toothpick inserted near the center comes out clean. Cool for 10 minutes before removing from pans to wire racks to cool completely. **Yield:** 3 loaves.

Banana Nut Bread — *Susan Jones, La Grange Park, Illinois*

1/4 cup butter, softened
3/4 cup sugar
2 eggs
3/4 cup mashed ripe bananas
    (about 2 medium)
1/2 cup sour cream
2-1/4 cups all-purpose flour
1 teaspoon ground cinnamon
3/4 teaspoon baking soda
1/2 teaspoon salt
1/2 cup chopped walnuts

1. In a mixing bowl, cream the butter, sugar and eggs, mixing well. Stir in bananas and sour cream. Stir in dry ingredients just until moistened. Fold in nuts.

2. Pour into a greased 8-in. x 4-in. x 2-in. loaf pan. Bake at 350° for 1 hour or until a toothpick inserted near the center comes out clean. Cool in pan 10 minutes before removing to a wire rack. **Yield:** 1 loaf.

Bubble Bread Wreath —*Sylvia Petker, Port Rowan, Ontario*

2 tablespoons active dry yeast
1 tablespoon plus 1/2 cup sugar, *divided*
1 cup warm water (110° to 115°)
2 cups warm milk (110° to 115°)
1-2/3 cups butter, softened, *divided*
2 eggs, beaten
1 tablespoon salt
8 cups all-purpose flour
1 cup chopped red and green candied
   cherries, *divided*
1-1/3 cups chopped pecans, *divided*
SYRUP:
1 cup light corn syrup
6 tablespoons butter
2 teaspoons vanilla extract

1. In a large mixing bowl, dissolve yeast and 1 table-spoon sugar in water. Let stand for 5 minutes. Add milk, 2/3 cup butter, eggs, salt and remaining sugar. Stir in enough flour to form a soft dough.

2. Turn onto a floured surface; knead until smooth and elastic, about 6-8 minutes. Place in a greased bowl, turning once to grease top. Cover and let rise in a warm place until doubled, about 1 hour.

3. Punch dough down; shape into 1-1/2-in. balls. Divide half of the balls between two greased 10-in. fluted tube pans. In each pan, arrange 1/4 cup cherries in spaces between balls; sprinkle with about 1/3 cup pecans. Melt the remaining butter; drizzle 1/4 cup over each pan. Repeat the layers once. Cover and let rise until nearly doubled, about 30 minutes.

4. Bake at 350° for 30-35 minutes or until golden brown. Meanwhile, in a saucepan, heat syrup ingredients. Slowly drizzle over warm loaves. Cool for 10 minutes before inverting onto wire racks. **Yield:** 2 loaves.

Walnut Cream Braid —*Jean Erickson, North Pole, Alaska*

1 package (1/4 ounce) active dry yeast
1/4 cup warm water (110° to 115°)
1/2 cup butter, softened
2 tablespoons sugar
1/2 teaspoon salt
1 egg
2 to 2-1/2 cups all-purpose flour
FILLING:
2 packages (3 ounces *each*) cream
   cheese, softened
3/4 cup sugar
1/2 cup finely chopped walnuts
Confectioners' sugar

1. In a mixing bowl, dissolve yeast in water. Add butter, sugar, salt, egg and 1-1/2 cups flour; beat on low for 3 minutes, scraping bowl occasionally. Stir in enough remaining flour to form a soft dough.

2. Turn onto a floured surface; knead until smooth and elastic, about 6-8 minutes. Place in a greased bowl, turning once to grease top. Cover and let rise in a warm place until doubled, about 1 hour. Meanwhile, in a small mixing bowl, beat the cream cheese and sugar; set aside.

3. Punch dough down; divide in half. On a floured surface, roll each portion into a 12-in. x 8-in. rectangle and place on greased baking sheets. Spread half of the filling down the center third of each rectangle. Sprinkle with walnuts. On each long side, cut 1-in.-wide strips about 2-1/2 in. into center. Starting at one end, fold alternating strips at an angle across filling. Seal ends. Cover and let rise for 30 minutes.

4. Bake at 375° for 15-20 minutes or until browned. Cool on wire racks. Dust with confectioners' sugar if desired. **Yield:** 2 loaves.

Top to bottom: Bubble
Bread Wreath, Rosemary
Jelly (recipe on p. 183)
and Walnut Cream Braid.

Pineapple Cherry Loaves –*Dolores Peltier, Warren, Michigan*

1-3/4 cups butter, softened
2 cups sugar
8 eggs
1 teaspoon vanilla extract
3-3/4 cups all-purpose flour
1 teaspoon salt
1 teaspoon baking powder
2 cans (8 ounces *each*) pineapple chunks, drained
1 jar (10 ounces) red maraschino cherries, drained and halved
1 jar (10 ounces) green maraschino cherries, drained and halved
2 cups chopped walnuts

1. In a mixing bowl, cream butter and sugar. Add eggs, one at a time, beating well after each addition. Beat in vanilla. Combine the flour, salt and baking powder; add to creamed mixture until well blended. Stir in pineapple, cherries and nuts. Pour into three greased and floured 8-in. x 4-in. x 2-in. loaf pans.

2. Bake at 325° for 1-1/4 hours or until a toothpick inserted near the center comes out clean. Cool for 10 minutes before removing from pans to wire racks. Yield: 3 loaves.

Walnut Marmalade Mini Loaves *–Michele Bragg, Palm City, Florida*

2-1/2 cups all-purpose flour
1/3 cup sugar
1 tablespoon baking powder
1 teaspoon salt
1 jar (12 ounces) orange marmalade
1 cup orange juice
3 tablespoons vegetable oil
1 egg
1 cup chopped walnuts

1. In a mixing bowl, combine the flour, sugar, baking powder and salt. Combine the marmalade, orange juice, oil and egg; stir into dry ingredients just until moistened. Stir in walnuts. Pour into three greased 5-3/4-in. x 3-in. x 2-in. loaf pans.

2. Bake at 350° for 40-50 minutes or until a toothpick inserted near the center comes out clean. Cool for 10 minutes before removing from pans to wire racks. **Yield:** 3 loaves.

Golden Knots *–Pat Habiger, Spearville, Kansas*

2 packages (1/4 ounce *each*) active dry yeast
2 tablespoons plus 1 cup sugar, *divided*
1-1/2 cups warm water (110° to 115°), *divided*
1 cup milk
1/2 cup butter
2 eggs
2 teaspoons salt
8-1/2 to 9 cups all-purpose flour
Melted butter

1. In a large mixing bowl, dissolve yeast and 2 tablespoons sugar in 1/2 cup water. In a saucepan, heat the milk, butter and remaining water to 110°-115°; add to yeast mixture. Add eggs, salt, 5 cups flour and the remaining sugar; beat until smooth. Add enough of the remaining flour to form a soft dough.

2. Turn onto a floured surface; knead until smooth and elastic, about 6-8 minutes. Place in a greased bowl, turning once to grease top. Cover and let rise in a warm place until doubled, about 1 hour.

3. Punch dough down. Divide into thirds; roll each portion into a 14-in. roll. Divide each roll into 14 pieces. Roll pieces into 9-in. ropes and tie into knots. Place the rolls 2 in. apart on greased baking sheets. Cover and let rise until doubled, about 30 minutes.

4. Bake at 350° for 15-20 minutes or until golden brown. Brush with melted butter. **Yield:** 3-1/2 dozen.

Cinnamon Swirl Loaves —*Lynn Callahan, Rosemount, Minnesota*

1/3 **cup shortening**
1-1/2 **cups plus 2 tablespoons sugar,** *divided*
3 **eggs**
1-1/2 **teaspoons vanilla extract**
3 **cups all-purpose flour**
1-1/2 **teaspoons baking powder**
3/4 **teaspoon baking soda**
3/4 **teaspoon salt**
1-1/2 **cups buttermilk**
1 **tablespoon ground cinnamon**

1. In a large mixing bowl, cream shortening and 1-1/2 cups sugar. Add eggs, one at a time, beating well after each addition. Beat in vanilla. Combine the flour, baking powder, baking soda and salt; add to creamed mixture alternately with buttermilk.

2. Spread half of the batter in two greased and floured 8-in. x 4-in. x 2-in. loaf pans. Combine cinnamon and remaining sugar; sprinkle half over batter. Spread with the remaining batter; sprinkle with remaining cinnamon-sugar.

3. Bake at 350° for 50-55 minutes or until a toothpick inserted near the center comes out clean. Cool for 10 minutes before removing from pans to wire racks. **Yield:** 2 loaves.

Accordion Rye Rolls —*Alyson Armstrong, Parkersburg, West Virginia*

2 **packages (1/4 ounce** *each***) active dry yeast**
1/2 **cup warm water (110° to 115°)**
1-1/2 **cups warm milk (110° to 115°)**
1/4 **cup molasses**
4 **tablespoons butter, softened,** *divided*
1 **tablespoon sugar**
1 **tablespoon plus 1/2 teaspoon salt,** *divided*
3 **to 3-1/2 cups all-purpose flour**
2-1/2 **cups rye flour**
Vegetable oil
1 **egg white**
2 **teaspoons caraway seeds**

1. In a large mixing bowl, dissolve yeast in warm water. Add the milk, molasses, 2 tablespoons butter, sugar and 1 tablespoon salt. Add 2 cups all-purpose flour; beat until smooth. Stir in rye flour and enough remaining all-purpose flour to form a soft dough.

2. Turn onto a floured surface; knead until smooth and elastic, about 6-8 minutes. Place in a greased bowl, turning once to grease top. Cover and let rest for 20 minutes.

3. Punch dough down. Turn onto a lightly floured surface; divide into four portions. Roll out each portion into a 14-in. x 6-in. rectangle. Brush with the remaining butter.

4. With dull edge of a table knife, score dough widthwise at 2-in. intervals. Using those marks as a guideline, make score marks widthwise across the dough. Fold dough accordion-style back and forth along creased lines. Cut folded dough into 1-in. pieces. Place each piece cut side down in a greased muffin cup. Brush with oil. Cover loosely with plastic wrap. Refrigerate for 4-24 hours.

5. When ready to bake, uncover dough and let stand at room temperature for 10 minutes. In a small mixing bowl, beat egg white until stiff peaks form; brush over dough. Sprinkle with caraway seeds and remaining salt. Bake at 375° for 20-25 minutes or until lightly browned. Remove from pans to wire racks. **Yield:** 2 dozen.

Autumn Pear Bread *–Mary Lynn Wilson, Linden, Texas*

2 cups all-purpose flour
1 cup sugar
1 teaspoon baking powder
1/2 teaspoon baking soda
1/2 teaspoon salt
1/8 teaspoon ground nutmeg
1/2 cup butter
2 eggs
1/4 cup buttermilk
1 teaspoon vanilla extract
1 cup finely chopped peeled ripe pears

1. In a large bowl, combine dry ingredients; cut in butter until mixture resembles coarse crumbs. In a small bowl, beat eggs, buttermilk and vanilla; stir into dry ingredients just until moistened. Fold in the pears. Spoon into three greased 5-in. x 2-1/2-in. x 2-in. mini-loaf pans.

2. Bake at 350° for 35-40 minutes or until a toothpick inserted near the center comes out clean. Cool in pans 10 minutes before removing to wire racks to cool completely. **Yield:** 3 mini loaves.

Cherry Banana Mini Loaves *–Diane Doll, West Bend, Wisconsin*

1/2 cup butter, softened
1 cup sugar
2 eggs
1 cup mashed bananas
   (about 2 medium)
2 cups all-purpose flour
1 teaspoon baking soda
1/4 cup chopped walnuts
1/4 cup miniature semisweet chocolate
   chips
1/4 cup dried cherries *or* cranberries

1. In a mixing bowl, cream butter and sugar. Add eggs and banana; mix well. Combine flour and baking soda; gradually add to creamed mixture. Fold in the nuts, chips and cherries. Transfer to four greased 5-3/4-in. x 3-in. x 2-in. loaf pans.

2. Bake at 350° for 32-37 minutes or until a toothpick inserted near the center comes out clean. Cool for 10 minutes before removing from pans to wire racks. **Yield:** 4 loaves.

Berry Mini Breads —*Heidi Naylor, Boise, Idaho*

1/2 cup butter, softened
1 cup sugar
2 eggs
3 cups all-purpose flour
1 teaspoon baking soda
1 teaspoon baking powder
1 teaspoon salt
1 cup buttermilk
1 cup whole-berry cranberry sauce
1 cup fresh *or* frozen blueberries

1. In a mixing bowl, cream butter and sugar. Add the eggs, one at a time, beating well after each addition. Combine dry ingredients; add to the creamed mixture alternately with buttermilk. Stir in cranberry sauce and blueberries. Pour into four greased 5-3/4-in. x 3-in. x 2-in. loaf pans.

2. Bake at 350° for 25-30 minutes or until a toothpick inserted near the center comes out clean. Cool for 10 minutes before removing from pans to wire racks. **Yield:** 4 loaves.

Tropical Sweet Bread —*Camie Schuiteman, Marion, Indiana*

1/4 cup warm buttermilk (70° to 80°)
1/4 cup pineapple juice
3 tablespoons butter, softened
1 egg
1/2 cup pineapple tidbits
1/2 cup sliced ripe banana
3 cups bread flour
1/4 cup whole wheat flour
1/2 cup flaked coconut
4-1/2 teaspoons sugar
1 teaspoon salt
1/4 teaspoon baking soda
1-1/2 teaspoons active dry yeast
1/3 cup chopped macadamia nuts

1. In bread machine pan, place the first 13 ingredients in order suggested by manufacturer. Select basic bread setting. Choose crust color and loaf size if available. Bake according to bread machine directions (check dough after 5 minutes of mixing; add 1 to 2 tablespoons water or flour if needed).

2. Just before the final kneading (your machine may audibly signal this), add the macadamia nuts. **Yield:** 1 loaf (2 pounds).

Editor's Note: Warmed buttermilk will appear curdled. If your bread machine has a time-delay feature, we recommend you do not use it for this recipe.

Paradise Buns —*Liz Lazenby, Victoria, British Columbia*

1 loaf (1 pound) frozen bread dough, thawed
1 cup (4 ounces) shredded cheddar cheese
1/4 cup *each* diced mushrooms, broccoli and sweet red and yellow pepper
1 tablespoon chopped green onion
1 garlic clove, minced
1/2 teaspoon garlic powder

1. Divide bread dough into eight pieces. In a bowl, combine the cheese, vegetables, garlic and garlic powder. Roll each piece of dough into an 8-in. rope. Roll in cheese mixture, pressing mixture into dough. Tie into a knot and press vegetables into dough; tuck ends under.

2. Place 2 in. apart on greased baking sheets. Cover and let rise until doubled, about 30 minutes. Bake at 375° for 15-20 minutes or until golden brown. **Yield:** 8 servings.

Berry Mini Breads

Sugarplum Spice Bread —*Jackie Brown, Tully, New York*

3/4 cup butter, softened
3/4 cup sugar
4 eggs
5-1/2 to 6 cups all-purpose flour
2 packages (1/4 ounce *each*) quick-rise yeast
1-1/2 teaspoons ground cardamom
1 teaspoon salt
3/4 teaspoon ground cinnamon
1/4 teaspoon ground nutmeg
1-1/2 cups milk
1 cup diced dried fruit
1/2 cup raisins
1/2 cup golden raisins
FROSTING:
2 tablespoons butter, softened
2 tablespoons shortening
2 cups confectioners' sugar
1/2 teaspoon vanilla extract
2 to 3 tablespoons milk

1. In a large mixing bowl, cream butter and sugar. Add eggs, one at a time, beating well after each addition. Add 4 cups flour, yeast, cardamom, salt, cinnamon and nutmeg. Heat milk to 120°-130°; add to creamed mixture and beat until moistened. Stir in enough remaining flour to form a firm dough.

2. Turn onto a heavily floured surface. Sprinkle with fruit and raisins; knead until smooth and elastic, about 6-8 minutes. Cover and let rise in a warm place until doubled, about 40 minutes.

3. Punch dough down. Turn onto a lightly floured surface; divide into eight portions. Shape into loaves. Place in eight greased 5-3/4-in. x 3-in. x 2-in. loaf pans. Cover and let rise until doubled, about 30 minutes. Bake at 350° for 30-35 minutes or until golden brown. Remove from pans to wire racks to cool.

4. For frosting, in a small mixing bowl, cream butter and shortening. Gradually beat in confectioners' sugar, vanilla and enough milk to achieve spreading consistency. Frost loaves. **Yield:** 8 mini loaves.

Blueberry Banana Bread –*Sandy Flick, Toledo, Ohio*

2 cups all-purpose flour
1 teaspoon baking soda
1/2 teaspoon salt
1/2 cup shortening
1 cup sugar
2 eggs
2 teaspoons vanilla extract
2 medium ripe bananas, mashed
1 cup fresh blueberries

1. In a bowl, combine the flour, baking soda and salt. In a large mixing bowl, cream the shortening and sugar. Add eggs and vanilla; mix well. Beat in bananas. Gradually add the dry ingredients, beating just until combined. Fold in blueberries. Pour into three greased 5-3/4-in. x 3-in. x 2-in. loaf pans.

2. Bake at 350° for 30-35 minutes or until a toothpick inserted near the center comes out clean. Cool for 10 minutes before removing from pans to wire racks. **Yield:** 3 mini loaves.

Hazelnut Swirl Bread –*Loraine Meyer, Bend, Oregon*

2 packages (1/4 ounce *each*) active dry yeast
1/2 cup warm water (110° to 115°)
2 cups warm milk (110° to 115°)
1 cup mashed potato flakes
2/3 cup shortening
1/2 cup sugar
2 eggs, lightly beaten
1 teaspoon salt
3 cups whole wheat flour
3 to 4 cups all-purpose flour
FILLING:
3 tablespoons butter, softened
2/3 cup packed brown sugar
2 egg yolks
2 tablespoons milk
1/4 teaspoon vanilla extract
2 cups finely chopped hazelnuts

1. In a large mixing bowl, dissolve yeast in warm water. Add the milk, potato flakes, shortening, sugar, eggs, salt, whole wheat flour and 1 cup all-purpose flour; beat until smooth. Stir in enough remaining all-purpose flour to form a stiff dough.

2. Turn onto a floured surface; knead until smooth and elastic, about 6-8 minutes. Place in a greased bowl, turning once to grease top. Cover and let rise in a warm place until doubled, about 1 hour. Punch dough down. Turn onto a lightly floured surface; divide in half. Roll each portion into a 14-in. x 9-in. rectangle.

3. For filling, in a small mixing bowl, beat butter, brown sugar and egg yolks until creamy. Add milk and vanilla; mix well. Stir in hazelnuts. Spread over dough to within 1/2 in. of edges. Roll up jelly-roll style, starting with a short side; pinch seams to seal. Place seam side down in two greased 9-in. x 5-in. x 3-in. loaf pans. Cover and let rise in a warm place until doubled, about 30 minutes.

4. Bake at 375° for 15 minutes. Cover with foil. Bake 20-25 minutes longer or until golden brown. Remove from pans to wire racks to cool. **Yield:** 2 loaves.

Chocolate Yeast Bread –*Laura Cryts, Derry, New Hampshire*

4-1/2 cups all-purpose flour
1/3 cup baking cocoa
2 tablespoons sugar
1 package (1/4 ounce) active dry yeast
1 teaspoon salt
1/4 teaspoon baking soda
1 cup water
1/2 cup milk
1/2 cup semisweet chocolate chips
2 tablespoons butter
1 egg

1. In a mixing bowl, combine 1-1/4 cups flour, cocoa, sugar, yeast, salt and baking soda. In a saucepan, heat the water, milk, chocolate chips and butter; stir until chocolate is melted. Cool to 120°-130°. Add to dry ingredients; beat on medium speed for 2 minutes. Add 1/2 cup flour and egg; beat on high for 2 minutes. Stir in enough remaining flour to form a stiff dough.

2. Turn onto a floured surface; knead until smooth and elastic, about 6-8 minutes. Place in a greased bowl, turning once to grease top. Cover and let rise in a warm place until doubled, about 1 hour.

3. Punch dough down. Turn onto a lightly floured surface; divide in half. Shape into loaves. Place in two greased 8-in. x 4-in. x 2-in. loaf pans. Cover and let rise until doubled, about 1 hour.

4. Bake at 375° for 25-30 minutes or until browned. Remove from pans to cool on wire racks. **Yield:** 2 loaves.

Cardamom Braids –*Sally Nelson, Tempe, Arizona*

2 packages (1/4 ounce *each*) active dry yeast
1/2 cup warm water (110° to 115°)
1-1/2 cups warm milk (110° to 115°)
1-1/2 cups sugar
1/2 cup butter, softened
3 eggs
2 teaspoons ground cardamom
1/2 teaspoon salt
9 to 10 cups all-purpose flour
Additional sugar

1. In a mixing bowl, dissolve yeast in warm water. Add warm milk, sugar, butter, 2 eggs, cardamom, salt and 6 cups flour; beat until smooth. Stir in enough remaining flour to form a soft dough.

2. Turn onto a floured surface; knead until smooth and elastic, about 6-8 minutes. Place in a greased bowl, turning once to grease top. Cover and let rise in a warm place until doubled, about 1-1/4 hours.

3. Punch dough down; cover and let rest for 10 minutes. Divide into fourths. Divide each portion into thirds; shape each into a 12-in. rope. Place three ropes on a greased baking sheet and braid; pinch ends to seal and tuck under. Repeat with remaining dough. Cover and let rise in a warm place until nearly doubled, about 45 minutes.

4. Beat remaining egg; brush over loaves. Sprinkle with additional sugar. Bake at 375° for 20-25 minutes or until golden brown. Remove from pans to wire racks. **Yield:** 4 loaves.

Braiding Bread

1. Place three ropes of dough almost touching on a baking sheet. Starting in the middle, loosely bring the left rope under the center rope. Bring the right rope under the new center rope and repeat until you reach the end.

2. Turn the pan and repeat braiding.

3. Press ends to seal; tuck under.

Gifts from the Country Kitchen

Cardamom Braids

Cardamon Cinnamon Knots –*Vivian Donner, Jackson, Michigan*

2 packages (1/4 ounce *each*) active dry yeast
1 cup warm water (110° to 115°)
1/2 teaspoon plus 2/3 cup sugar, *divided*
1-1/3 cups warm milk (110° to 115°)
2/3 cup butter, cubed
1/3 cup shortening
2 eggs, beaten
3/4 teaspoon salt
2 teaspoons cardamom seeds, crushed
8 to 8-1/2 cups all-purpose flour
1/4 cup ground cinnamon
ICING:
2 cups confectioners' sugar
5 tablespoons milk
1 tablespoon butter, melted
1/4 teaspoon vanilla extract

1. In a large mixing bowl, dissolve yeast in warm water. Add 1/2 teaspoon sugar; let stand for 5 minutes. Add the warm milk, butter, shortening, eggs, salt, cardamom, remaining sugar and 5 cups of flour. Beat until smooth. Stir in enough remaining flour to form a soft dough.

2. Turn onto a floured surface; knead until smooth and elastic, about 6-8 minutes. Place in a greased bowl, turning once to grease top. Cover and let rise in a warm place until doubled, about 1 hour.

3. Punch dough down. Turn onto a lightly floured surface; divide in half. Shape each portion into 18 balls. Roll each into an 8-in. rope; coat with cinnamon. Tie in a knot and tuck ends under. Place 2 in. apart on greased baking sheets. Cover and let rise until doubled, about 30 minutes.

4. Bake at 375° for 15-20 minutes or until golden brown. Remove from pans to wire racks. Combine icing ingredients; drizzle over rolls. **Yield:** 3 dozen.

Italian Sweet Bread –*Kathleen Schweichs, Lockport, Illinois*

1 cup milk
1 cup sugar
1 cup butter, cubed
1 cup raisins
2 packages (1/4 ounce *each*) active dry yeast
1/2 cup warm water (110° to 115°)
4 eggs
6 teaspoons anise extract
2 teaspoons vanilla extract
1 cup chopped walnuts
1/2 cup chopped red and green candied cherries
8 cups all-purpose flour
ICING:
1 cup confectioners' sugar
4 teaspoons milk

1. In a saucepan, combine the first four ingredients. Cook and stir over medium heat until butter is melted. Remove from the heat; cool to 110°-115°.

2. In a mixing bowl, dissolve yeast in warm water. Add the cooled butter mixture, eggs, extracts, nuts and cherries; mix well. Add enough flour to form a soft dough.

3. Turn onto a floured surface; knead until smooth and elastic, about 6-8 minutes. Place in a greased bowl, turning once to grease top. Cover and let rise in a warm place until doubled, about 1 hour.

4. Punch dough down; divide into thirds. Shape each portion into an oval loaf; place in three greased and floured 8-in. x 4-in. x 2-in. baking pans. Cover and let rise until doubled, about 45 minutes.

5. Bake at 350° for 60-65 minutes or until golden brown. Cover loosely with foil if top browns too quickly. Remove from pans to wire racks to cool. Combine icing ingredients; drizzle over cooled loaves. **Yield:** 3 loaves.

Muffins, Scones & Pastries

Raspberry Chocolate Chip Muffins

—Carol Schwammel, Antioch, California

1-2/3 cups all-purpose flour
3/4 cup quick-cooking oats
2/3 cup sugar
2 teaspoons baking powder
1 teaspoon baking soda
1/4 teaspoon ground cinnamon
1 egg, lightly beaten
3/4 cup milk
1/3 cup vegetable oil
2 tablespoons orange juice
1 teaspoon vanilla extract
3/4 cup fresh *or* frozen unsweetened raspberries
1/2 cup miniature semisweet chocolate chips

1. In a large bowl, combine the first six ingredients. Combine egg, milk, oil, orange juice and vanilla; stir into dry ingredients just until moistened. Fold in raspberries and chocolate chips.

2. Fill greased or paper-lined muffin cups two-thirds full. Bake at 375° for 20-25 minutes or until a toothpick comes out clean. Cool for 5 minutes before removing from pan to a wire rack. **Yield:** 1 dozen.

Editor's Note: If using frozen berries, do not thaw before adding to batter.

Hazelnut Chip Scones *–Elisa Lochridge, Aloha, Oregon*

> 4 cups all-purpose flour
> 3 tablespoons sugar
> 4 teaspoons baking powder
> 1/2 teaspoon salt
> 1/2 teaspoon cream of tartar
> 3/4 cup cold butter
> 1 egg, *separated*
> 1-1/2 cups refrigerated hazelnut nondairy
>   creamer *or* half-and-half cream
> 1-1/2 cups semisweet chocolate chips
> Additional sugar
> **SPICED BUTTER:**
> 1/2 cup butter, softened
> 3 tablespoons brown sugar
> 1/4 teaspoon ground cinnamon
> 1/4 teaspoon ground allspice
> 1/8 teaspoon ground nutmeg

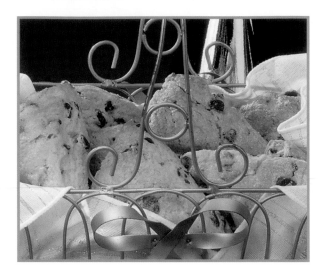

1. In a bowl, combine the first five ingredients; cut in butter until crumbly. In a bowl, whisk egg yolk and creamer; add to dry ingredients just until moistened. Stir in the chocolate chips.

2. Turn onto a floured surface; knead 10 times. Divide dough in half. Pat each portion into a 7-in. circle; cut into eight wedges. Separate wedges and place on greased baking sheets.

3. Beat egg white; brush over dough. Sprinkle with additional sugar. Bake at 425° for 15-18 minutes or until golden brown. Meanwhile, in a small mixing bowl, combine the spiced butter ingredients; beat until smooth. Serve with warm scones. **Yield:** 16 scones.

Lemon-Blueberry Oat Muffins *–Jamie Brown, Walden, Colorado*

> 1 cup quick-cooking oats
> 1 cup all-purpose flour
> 1/2 cup sugar
> 3 teaspoons baking powder
> 1/4 teaspoon salt
> 1 egg
> 1 egg white
> 1 cup milk
> 2 tablespoons butter, melted
> 1 teaspoon grated lemon peel
> 1 teaspoon vanilla extract
> 1 cup fresh *or* frozen blueberries
> **TOPPING:**
> 1/2 cup quick-cooking oats
> 2 tablespoons brown sugar
> 1 tablespoon butter, softened

1. In a bowl, combine the first five ingredients. In another bowl, combine the egg, egg white, milk, butter, lemon peel and vanilla. Add to dry ingredients just until moistened. Fold in berries.

2. Fill greased or paper-lined muffin cups two-thirds full with batter. Combine topping ingredients; sprinkle over batter. Bake at 400° for 20-22 minutes or until top is lightly browned and springs back when lightly touched. Cool for 5 minutes before removing from pan to a wire rack. **Yield:** 1 dozen.

Editor's Note: If using frozen blueberries, do not thaw before adding to the batter.

Cappuccino Muffins —*Janice Bassing, Racine, Wisconsin*

ESPRESSO SPREAD:
- 4 ounces cream cheese, cubed
- 1 tablespoon sugar
- 1/2 teaspoon instant coffee granules
- 1/2 teaspoon vanilla extract
- 1/4 cup miniature semisweet chocolate chips

MUFFINS:
- 2 cups all-purpose flour
- 3/4 cup sugar
- 2-1/2 teaspoons baking powder
- 1 teaspoon ground cinnamon
- 1/2 teaspoon salt
- 1 cup milk
- 2 tablespoons instant coffee granules
- 1/2 cup butter, melted
- 1 egg, beaten
- 1 teaspoon vanilla extract
- 3/4 cup miniature semisweet chocolate chips

1. In a food processor or blender, combine the spread ingredients; cover and process until well blended. Cover and refrigerate until serving.

2. In a bowl, combine flour, sugar, baking powder, cinnamon and salt. In another bowl, stir milk and coffee granules until coffee is dissolved. Add butter, egg and vanilla; mix well. Stir into dry ingredients just until moistened. Fold in chocolate chips.

3. Fill greased or paper-lined muffin cups two-thirds full. Bake at 375° for 17-20 minutes or until a toothpick comes out clean. Cool for 5 minutes before removing from pans to wire racks. Serve with espresso spread. **Yield:** about 14 muffins (1 cup spread).

Apple Bran Muffins —*Nancy Brown, Klamath Falls, Oregon*

- 2 large Golden Delicious apples, peeled and chopped
- 1/2 cup butter
- 3 cups All-Bran cereal
- 1 cup boiling water
- 2 cups buttermilk
- 2 eggs, lightly beaten
- 2/3 cup sugar
- 1 cup raisins
- 2-1/2 cups all-purpose flour
- 2-1/2 teaspoons baking soda
- 2 teaspoons ground cinnamon
- 1 teaspoon ground nutmeg
- 1/2 teaspoon ground cloves
- 1/2 teaspoon salt

1. In a skillet, saute apples in butter until tender, about 10 minutes. Combine cereal and water in a large bowl; stir in the buttermilk, eggs, sugar, raisins and apples with butter. Combine dry ingredients; stir into apple mixture just until moistened. Refrigerate in a tightly covered container for at least 24 hours (batter will be very thick).

2. Fill greased or paper-lined muffin cups three-fourths full. Bake at 400° for 20-25 minutes or until a toothpick comes out clean. Cool in pan 10 minutes before removing to a wire rack. **Yield:** about 24 muffins.

Editor's Note: Batter can be stored in a tightly covered container in the refrigerator for up to 2 weeks.

Trail Mix Muffins –*Patricia Jones, Hugo, Colorado*

2-1/4 cups all-purpose flour
   1 cup granola cereal without raisins
  3/4 cup packed brown sugar
   2 teaspoons baking powder
  1/2 teaspoon salt
   2 eggs
   1 cup milk
  3/4 cup vegetable oil
   1 teaspoon vanilla extract
  1/2 cup miniature semisweet chocolate chips
  1/2 cup chopped dry-roasted peanuts
  1/2 cup raisins
  1/2 cup chopped dried apricots

1. In a large bowl, combine the flour, cereal, brown sugar, baking powder and salt. In another bowl, beat the eggs, milk, oil and vanilla; stir into dry ingredients just until moistened. Fold in the chips, peanuts, raisins and apricots.

2. Fill greased or paper-lined muffin cups three-fourths full. Bake at 375° for 15-18 minutes or until a toothpick comes out clean. Cool for 5 minutes before removing from pans to wire racks. Serve warm. **Yield:** about 1-1/2 dozen.

Almond Bear Claws –*Aneta Kish, La Crosse, Wisconsin*

1-1/2 cups cold butter, cut into 1/2-inch pieces
   5 cups all-purpose flour, *divided*
   1 package (1/4 ounce) active dry yeast
1-1/4 cups half-and-half cream
  1/4 cup sugar
  1/4 teaspoon salt
   2 eggs
   1 egg white
  3/4 cup confectioners' sugar
  1/2 cup almond paste, cubed
   1 tablespoon water
Coarse *or* granulated sugar
Sliced almonds

1. In a bowl, toss butter with 3 cups flour until well coated; refrigerate. In a mixing bowl, combine yeast and remaining flour. In a saucepan, heat cream, sugar and salt to 120°-130°. Add to yeast mixture with 1 egg; mix well. Stir in butter mixture just until moistened.

2. Turn onto a lightly floured surface; knead 10 times. Roll into a 21-in. x 12-in. rectangle. Starting at a short side, fold dough in thirds, forming a 12-in. x 7-in. rectangle. Cover and chill for 1 hour.

3. For filling, in a mixing bowl, beat egg white until foamy. Gradually add confectioners' sugar and almond paste; beat until smooth. Cut dough in half widthwise. Roll each portion into a 12-in. square; cut each square into three 12-in. x 4-in. strips. Spread about 2 tablespoons filling down center of each strip. Fold long edges together; seal edges and ends. Cut into three pieces.

4. Place on greased baking sheets with folded edge facing away from you. With scissors, cut strips four times to within 1/2 in. of folded edge; separate slightly. Repeat with remaining dough and filling. Cover and let rise in a warm place until doubled, about 1 hour.

5. Lightly beat water and remaining egg; brush over dough. Sprinkle with sugar and almonds. Bake at 375° for 15 minutes or until golden brown. Remove from pans to wire racks to cool. **Yield:** 1-1/2 dozen.

Trail Mix Muffins

Cranberry Coffee Cake —*Doris Brearley, Vestal, New York*

2 cups biscuit/baking mix
2 tablespoons sugar
2/3 cup milk
1 egg, beaten
2/3 cup jellied cranberry sauce
TOPPING:
1/2 cup chopped walnuts
1/2 cup packed brown sugar
1/2 teaspoon ground cinnamon
GLAZE:
1 cup confectioners' sugar
2 tablespoons milk
1/4 teaspoon vanilla extract

1. In a large bowl, combine the biscuit mix, sugar, milk and egg. Pour into a greased 8-in. square baking dish. Drop cranberry sauce by teaspoonfuls over batter. Combine topping ingredients; sprinkle over cranberry sauce.

2. Bake at 400° for 18-23 minutes or until a toothpick inserted near the center comes out clean. Cool on a wire rack.

3. In a small bowl, combine the glaze ingredients; drizzle over coffee cake. **Yield:** 9 servings.

Fudgy Banana Muffins —*Kristin Wagner, Spokane, Washington*

1-1/4 cups all-purpose flour
1 cup whole wheat flour
3/4 cup packed brown sugar
1-1/2 teaspoons baking powder
1 teaspoon baking soda
1/4 teaspoon salt
3 medium ripe bananas, mashed
1-1/4 cups milk
1 egg
1 tablespoon vegetable oil
2 teaspoons vanilla extract
6 milk chocolate candy bars (1.55 ounces *each*)

1. In a mixing bowl, combine the flours, brown sugar, baking powder, baking soda and salt. In another bowl, combine bananas, milk, egg, oil and vanilla; stir into dry ingredients just until moistened.

2. Fill greased or paper-lined muffin cups one-third full. Break each candy bar into 12 pieces; place two pieces in each muffin cup. Top with remaining batter. Chop remaining candy bar pieces; sprinkle over batter.

3. Bake at 400° for 15 minutes or until toothpick comes out clean. Cool for 5 minutes before removing from pans to wire racks. **Yield:** 1-1/2 dozen.

State Fair Cream Puffs —*Ruth Jungbluth, Dodgeville, Wisconsin*

1 cup water
1/2 cup butter
1 cup all-purpose flour
1/4 teaspoon salt
4 eggs
2 tablespoons milk
1 egg yolk, lightly beaten
2 cups heavy whipping cream
1/4 cup confectioners' sugar
1/2 teaspoon vanilla extract
Additional confectioners' sugar

1. In a saucepan over medium heat, bring water and butter to a boil. Add flour and salt all at once; stir until a smooth ball forms. Remove from the heat; let stand for 5 minutes. Add eggs, one at a time, beating well after each addition. Beat until smooth.

2. Drop by 1/4 cupfuls 3 in. apart onto greased baking sheets. Combine milk and egg yolk; brush over puffs. Bake at 400° for 35 minutes or until golden brown. Remove to wire racks. Immediately cut a slit in each for steam to escape; cool.

3. In a mixing bowl, beat cream until it begins to thicken. Add sugar and vanilla; beat until almost stiff. Split puffs; remove soft dough. Fill the puffs just before serving. Dust with confectioners' sugar. Refrigerate leftovers. **Yield:** 10 servings.

Cranberry Pumpkin Muffins —*Sue Ross, Casa Grande, Arizona*

2-1/4 cups all-purpose flour
1 teaspoon baking soda
1 teaspoon pumpkin pie spice
1/2 teaspoon salt
2 eggs
2 cups sugar
1 cup canned pumpkin
1/2 cup vegetable oil
1 cup fresh *or* frozen cranberries,
   chopped

1. In a large bowl, combine the first four ingredients. In a mixing bowl, beat the eggs and sugar; add the pumpkin and oil and mix well. Stir into the dry ingredients just until moistened. Fold in the cranberries.

2. Fill foil- or paper-lined muffin cups three-fourths full. Bake at 400° for 18-22 minutes or until a toothpick comes out clean. Cool for 5 minutes before removing from pans to wire racks. **Yield:** 2 dozen.

Blueberry Cheese Danish —Taste of Home Test Kitchen

3/4 cup cottage cheese
1/3 cup sugar
1/3 cup milk
1/4 cup vegetable oil
1 teaspoon vanilla extract
2 cups all-purpose flour
2 teaspoons baking powder
1/2 teaspoon salt
FILLING:
4 ounces cream cheese
1/4 cup sugar
1 egg, *separated*
1 teaspoon grated lemon peel
1 teaspoon vanilla extract
1 cup fresh *or* frozen blueberries
1 tablespoon water
GLAZE:
1/2 cup confectioners' sugar
2 teaspoons lemon juice

1. In a blender or food processor, cover and process cottage cheese until smooth. Add sugar, milk, oil and vanilla; cover and process until smooth. Combine the flour, baking powder and salt; add to cheese mixture. Cover and process just until dough forms a ball (dough will be sticky). Turn onto a floured surface; knead 4-5 times. Place in a bowl; cover and refrigerate for 30 minutes.

2. In a mixing bowl, beat cream cheese and sugar until smooth. Add egg yolk, lemon peel and vanilla; mix well. Turn dough onto a 17-in. x 13-in. piece of parchment paper. Roll into a 16-in. x 12-in. rectangle. Transfer with paper to a baking sheet.

3. Spread cream cheese mixture lengthwise in a 3-1/2-in.-wide strip down center of dough; sprinkle with blueberries. On each long side, cut 1-in.-wide strips about 3-3/4 in. into center. Fold alternating strips at an angle across berries. Pinch ends to seal and tuck under. Beat egg white and water; brush over dough.

4. Bake at 400° for 20-22 minutes or until golden brown. Remove to a wire rack. Combine glaze ingredients; drizzle over warm pastry. Refrigerate leftovers.
Yield: 10 servings.

Editor's Note: If using frozen blueberries, do not thaw.

Snappy Ginger Muffins —*Marlene Falsetti, Lowbanks, Ontario*

1/2 cup vegetable oil
1/4 cup sugar
1/4 cup packed brown sugar
1 cup molasses
1 egg
3 cups all-purpose flour
1-1/2 teaspoons baking soda
1 teaspoon ground cinnamon
1 teaspoon ground ginger
1/2 teaspoon salt
1 cup water

1. In a mixing bowl, beat the oil and sugars. Beat in molasses and egg. Combine the flour, baking soda, cinnamon, ginger and salt; stir into molasses mixture alternately with water.

2. Fill greased or paper-lined muffin cups two-thirds full. Bake at 350° for 20-25 minutes or until a toothpick comes out clean. Cool in pan for 10 minutes before removing to a wire racks. **Yield:** about 20 muffins.

Mini Apricot Turnovers —*Taste of Home Test Kitchen*

1 package (15 ounces) refrigerated pie pastry
1 jar (12 ounces) apricot *or* peach preserves
2 tablespoons milk
1 tablespoon sugar
1/4 teaspoon ground cinnamon

1. Cut each pastry into four wedges. Place a rounded tablespoonful of preserves in the center of each. Moisten edges with water. Fold pastry over filling; press edges with fork to seal.

2. Place turnovers on an ungreased baking sheet. Cut a small slit in the top of each. Brush with milk. Combine sugar and cinnamon; sprinkle over turnovers. Bake at 425° for 16-18 minutes or until golden brown. Serve warm. **Yield:** 8 turnovers.

Chocolate Eclairs *—Janet Davis, Murfreesboro, Tennessee*

1/2 cup butter
1 cup water
1/4 teaspoon salt
1 cup all-purpose flour
4 eggs
FILLING:
1 package (5.1 ounces) instant vanilla pudding mix
2-1/2 cups cold milk
1 cup heavy whipping cream
1/4 cup confectioners' sugar
1 teaspoon vanilla extract
CHOCOLATE ICING:
2 squares (1 ounce *each*) semisweet chocolate
2 tablespoons butter
1 cup confectioners' sugar
2 to 3 tablespoons hot water

1. In a saucepan, bring butter, water and salt to a boil. Add flour all at once; stir until a smooth ball forms. Remove from heat; let stand 5 minutes. Add eggs, one at a time, beating well after each addition. Continue beating until mixture is smooth and shiny.

2. With a tablespoon or a pastry tube fitted with a No. 10 or larger tip, spoon or pipe dough into 4-in.-long x 1-1/2-in.-wide strips on a greased baking sheet. Bake at 450° for 15 minutes. Reduce heat to 325°; bake 20 minutes longer. Cool on a wire rack.

3. For filling, combine pudding mix and milk; mix according to package directions. In another bowl, whip cream until soft peaks form. Beat in sugar and vanilla; fold into pudding. Fill cooled shells. (Chill remaining pudding for another use.)

4. For icing, melt chocolate and butter in a saucepan over low heat. Stir in sugar. Add hot water until icing is smooth and reaches desired consistency. Cool slightly. Spread over eclairs. Chill until serving. **Yield:** 8-9 servings.

Oatmeal Carrot Muffins *—Jane Richter, Pompano Beach, Florida*

1 cup old-fashioned oats
1/2 cup raisins
1 cup milk
1/2 cup shredded carrot
1/2 cup sugar
1/2 cup packed brown sugar
1/4 cup vegetable oil
2 egg whites
1 teaspoon grated orange peel
1/2 cup all-purpose flour
1/2 cup whole wheat flour
1 tablespoon baking powder
1/2 teaspoon baking soda

1. In a large bowl, combine oats, raisins and milk. Cover and refrigerate 2 hours or overnight.

2. Combine carrot, sugars, oil, egg whites and orange peel; stir into oat mixture. Combine dry ingredients; stir into the batter just until moistened.

3. Fill greased or paper-lined muffin cups two-thirds full. Bake at 400° for 20-25 minutes or until a toothpick comes out clean done. Cool in pan 10 minutes before removing to a wire rack. **Yield:** 10 muffins.

Chocolate Eclairs

Cinnamon Crisps —*Sarah Bueckert, Austin, Manitoba*

4 cups all-purpose flour, *divided*
1 package (1/4 ounce) active dry yeast
1-1/4 cups warm milk (120° to 130°)
1/4 cup shortening
1/4 cup sugar
1 teaspoon salt
1 egg
FILLING:
1/2 cup packed brown sugar
1/2 cup sugar
1/4 cup butter, melted
1 teaspoon ground cinnamon
TOPPING:
1 cup sugar
1 teaspoon ground cinnamon
1/2 cup chopped pecans
1/4 cup butter, melted

1. In a mixing bowl, combine 2 cups flour and yeast. Combine milk, shortening, sugar and salt; add to flour mixture and beat for 1 minute. Add egg; beat on low speed for 1 minute. Beat on medium for 3 minutes. Add enough remaining flour to form a soft dough.

2. Turn onto a floured surface; knead until smooth and elastic, about 6-8 minutes. Place in a greased bowl, turning once to grease top. Cover and let rise in a warm place until doubled, about 1 hour. Meanwhile, combine filling ingredients; set aside. For topping, combine sugar, cinnamon and pecans; set aside.

3. Punch dough down; divide in half. On a floured surface, roll one portion into a 12-in. square. Spread with half of the filling. Roll up tightly and pinch to seal. Cut into 1-in. slices and place on greased baking sheets (four slices per sheet).

4. Cover with waxed paper; flatten slices with palm of hand into 3-in. circles. Repeat with remaining dough and filling. Cover and let rise until doubled, about 30 minutes. Cover with waxed paper and flatten or roll to 5-in. diameter. Brush with butter; sprinkle with topping. Cover with waxed paper; roll or flatten again. Bake at 400° for 10-12 minutes or until browned. **Yield:** 2 dozen.

Basil Cheddar Scones —*Taste of Home Test Kitchen*

2-1/4 cups all-purpose flour
2 teaspoons baking powder
1/2 cup cold butter, cubed
1 egg
1 cup milk
1 cup (4 ounces) shredded cheddar cheese
1/4 cup prepared pesto sauce

1. In a bowl, combine the flour and baking powder. Cut in butter until mixture resembles coarse crumbs. In another bowl, combine the egg, milk, cheese and pesto. Stir into flour mixture just until moistened.

2. Turn onto a lightly floured surface; knead 8-10 times. Transfer to a greased baking sheet. Pat into a 10-in. circle; cut into eight wedges but do not separate. Bake at 400° for 20-25 minutes or until golden brown. Serve warm. **Yield:** 8 scones.

Poppy Seed Lemonade Muffins —*Karen Ann Bland, Gove, Kansas*

2 cups all-purpose flour
9 tablespoons sugar, *divided*
4 teaspoons poppy seeds
3 teaspoons baking powder
1/2 teaspoon salt
3/4 cup lemonade concentrate, *divided*
1/2 cup milk
1/3 cup butter, melted
1 egg

1. In a large bowl, combine the flour, 5 tablespoons sugar, poppy seeds, baking powder and salt. In another bowl, combine 1/2 cup lemonade concentrate, milk, butter and egg until blended. Stir into dry ingredients just until combined.

2. Fill greased or paper-lined muffin cups three-fourths full. Bake at 400° for 15-20 minutes or until a toothpick comes out clean. Cool for 5 minutes before removing from pan to a wire rack.

3. In a small bowl, combine the remaining sugar and lemonade concentrate. Pierce muffin tops several times with a fork; drizzle with lemonade mixture. **Yield:** 1 dozen.

Three-Grain Muffins –*Dorothy Collins, Winnsboro, Texas*

2 cups quick-cooking oats
2 cups crushed Shredded Wheat
(about 4 large)
2 cups All-Bran
1 quart buttermilk
1 cup boiling water
1 cup vegetable oil
4 eggs, beaten
2-1/4 cups packed brown sugar
5 cups all-purpose flour
5 teaspoons baking soda
1 teaspoon salt

1. In a large bowl, combine oats, Shredded Wheat and bran. Add buttermilk, water, oil and eggs; stir for 1 minute. Stir in the brown sugar. Combine flour, baking soda and salt; add to the cereal mixture and stir well.

2. Fill greased or paper-lined muffin cups two-thirds full. Bake at 400° for 18-20 minutes. Cool for 10 minutes before removing from pans to wire racks. **Yield:** 4 dozen.

Editor's Note: Muffin batter can be stored in the refrigerator for up to 1 week.

Cinnamon Doughnut Muffins –*Sharon Pullen, Alvinston, Ontario*

1-3/4 cups all-purpose flour
1-1/2 teaspoons baking powder
1/2 teaspoon salt
1/2 teaspoon ground nutmeg
1/4 teaspoon ground cinnamon
3/4 cup sugar
1/3 cup vegetable oil
1 egg, lightly beaten
3/4 cup milk
Jam
TOPPING:
1/4 cup butter, melted
1/3 cup sugar
1 teaspoon ground cinnamon

1. In a large bowl, combine flour, baking powder, salt, nutmeg and cinnamon. Combine sugar, oil, egg and milk; stir into dry ingredients just until moistened.

2. Fill greased or paper-lined muffin cups half full; place 1 teaspoon jam on top. Cover jam with enough batter to fill muffin cups three-fourths full.

3. Bake at 350° for 20-25 minutes or until a toothpick comes out clean. Place melted butter in a small bowl; combine sugar and cinnamon in another bowl. Immediately after removing muffins from the oven, dip tops in butter, then in cinnamon-sugar. Serve warm. **Yield:** 10 muffins.

Sunshine Muffins –*Linnea Rein, Topeka, Kansas*

2 eggs
1/2 cup water
1/3 cup milk
2 tablespoons vegetable oil
1 package (9 ounces) yellow cake mix
1 package (8-1/2 ounces) corn bread/muffin mix

1. In a bowl, combine the eggs, water, milk and oil. Stir in mixes and mix well.

2. Fill greased and floured muffin cups half full. Bake at 350° for 18-22 minutes or until a toothpick comes out clean. Cool for 5 minutes before removing from pans to wire racks. **Yield:** 14 muffins.

Three-Grain Muffins

S'more Jumbo Muffins —*Pam Ivbuls, Omaha, Nebraska*

1-1/2 cups all-purpose flour
  1/2 cup graham cracker crumbs
     (about 8 squares)
  1/4 cup packed brown sugar
    1 teaspoon baking soda
  1/2 teaspoon salt
    1 egg
1-1/2 cups buttermilk
  1/4 cup vegetable oil
  3/4 cup semisweet chocolate chips
1-1/4 cups miniature marshmallows,
    divided

1. In a large bowl, combine the dry ingredients. Combine egg, buttermilk and oil; mix well. Stir into dry ingredients just until moistened. Fold in chocolate chips and 1 cup marshmallows.

2. Fill greased jumbo muffin cups three-fourths full. Sprinkle with remaining marshmallows. Bake at 375° for 18-20 minutes or until a toothpick comes out clean. Cool for 5 minutes before removing from pan to a wire rack. Serve warm. **Yield:** 6 muffins.

Candy Bar Croissants —*Beverly Sterling, Gasport, New York*

  1 tube (8 ounces) refrigerated crescent
    rolls
  1 tablespoon butter, softened
  2 plain milk chocolate candy bars (1.55
    ounces *each*), broken into small pieces
  1 egg, beaten
  2 tablespoons sliced almonds

1. Unroll crescent roll dough; separate into triangles. Brush with butter. Arrange candy bar pieces evenly over triangles; roll up from the wide end. Place point side down on a greased baking sheet; curve ends slightly. Brush with egg and sprinkle with almonds.

2. Bake at 375° for 11-13 minutes or until golden brown. Cool on a wire rack. **Yield:** 8 servings.

Casseroles

Lattice-Top Chicken Stew —*Janet Aselage, Sidney, Ohio*

1 package (16 ounces) frozen
  California-blend vegetables, thawed
  and drained
2 cups cubed cooked chicken
1 can (10-3/4 ounces) condensed cream
  of potato soup, undiluted
1 cup milk
1/2 cup shredded cheddar cheese
1/2 cup french-fried onions
1/2 teaspoon seasoned salt
1 tube (8 ounces) refrigerated crescent
  rolls

1. In a bowl, combine the vegetables, chicken, soup, milk, cheese, onions and seasoned salt. Transfer to a greased 13-in. x 9-in. x 2-in. baking dish. Bake, uncovered, at 350° for 20 minutes.

2. Meanwhile, separate crescent dough into two rectangles. Seal perforations; cut each rectangle lengthwise into four strips. Working quickly, weave strips over warm filling, forming a lattice crust. Bake 15 minutes longer or until the crust is golden brown. **Yield:** 6-8 servings.

Lasagna with White Sauce —Angie Price, Bradford, Tennessee

1 pound ground beef
1 large onion, chopped
1 can (14-1/2 ounces) diced tomatoes, undrained
2 tablespoons tomato paste
1 beef bouillon cube
1-1/2 teaspoons Italian seasoning
1 teaspoon salt
1/2 teaspoon pepper
1/4 teaspoon ground red *or* cayenne pepper

WHITE SAUCE:
2 tablespoons butter
3 tablespoons all-purpose flour
1 teaspoon salt
1/4 teaspoon pepper
2 cups milk
1-1/4 cups (6 ounces) shredded mozzarella cheese, *divided*
10 to 12 uncooked lasagna noodles

1. In a Dutch oven, cook beef and onion until meat is no longer pink and onion is tender; drain. Add tomatoes, tomato paste, bouillon and seasonings. Cover and cook over medium-low heat for 20 minutes, stirring occasionally.

2. Meanwhile, melt butter in a medium saucepan; stir in flour, salt and pepper. Add milk gradually; bring to a boil, stirring constantly. Reduce heat and cook for 1 minute. Remove from the heat and stir in half of the cheese; set aside.

3. Pour half of the meat sauce into an ungreased 13-in. x 9-in. x 2-in. baking dish. Cover with half of the lasagna noodles. Cover with remaining meat sauce. Top with remaining noodles. Pour white sauce over noodles. Sprinkle with remaining cheese. Cover and bake at 400° for 40 minutes or until noodles are done. **Yield:** 10-12 servings.

Cheesy Green Bean Casserole —Paula Magnus, Republic, Washington

1 package (16 ounces) frozen French-style green beans
2 cups diced fully cooked ham
2 cans (10-3/4 ounces *each*) condensed cream of celery soup, undiluted
1/2 cup mayonnaise
2 teaspoons Dijon mustard
2 cups (8 ounces) shredded cheddar cheese
1 cup (4 ounces) shredded mozzarella cheese
1/2 cup dry bread crumbs
2 tablespoons butter, melted

1. In an ungreased 13-in. x 9-in. x 2-in. baking dish, layer the green beans and ham. Combine the soup, mayonnaise and mustard; pour over ham. Sprinkle with cheeses. Toss bread crumbs and butter; sprinkle over the top.

2. Bake, uncovered, at 350° for 25-30 minutes or until heated through and cheese is melted. **Yield:** 8-10 servings.

Fancy Mac 'n' Cheese –Janet Twigg, Campbellford, Ontario

2 packages (7-1/4 ounces *each*) macaroni and white cheddar *or* cheddar cheese dinner mix
2 cups broccoli florets
1/2 cup chopped onion
2 garlic cloves, minced
1/2 cup plus 1 tablespoon butter, *divided*
1/2 cup milk
2 cups cubed fully cooked ham
1 tablespoon Dijon mustard
Salt and pepper to taste
1 cup soft bread crumbs
1/4 cup grated Parmesan cheese

1. Set cheese sauce packet from dinner mix aside. Bring 6 cups water to boil. Add macaroni; cook for 4 minutes. Add the broccoli, onion and garlic. Cook 3-6 minutes longer or until macaroni is tender; drain.

2. In a saucepan, melt 1/2 cup butter. Stir in cheese sauce mix and milk. Add ham, mustard, salt and pepper. Stir in macaroni mixture. Transfer to a greased broiler-proof 2-1/2-qt. baking dish.

3. Melt remaining butter; toss with bread crumbs and Parmesan cheese. Sprinkle over the top. Broil 4-6 in. from the heat for 4-5 minutes or until top is golden brown. **Yield:** 8 servings.

Twice-Baked Potato Casserole –Betty Miars, Anna, Ohio

6 medium unpeeled potatoes, baked
1/4 teaspoon salt
1/4 teaspoon pepper
1 pound sliced bacon, cooked and crumbled
3 cups (24 ounces) sour cream
2 cups (8 ounces) shredded mozzarella cheese
2 cups (8 ounces) shredded cheddar cheese
2 green onions, chopped

1. Cut baked potatoes into 1-in. cubes. Place half in a greased 13-in. x 9-in. x 2-in. baking dish. Sprinkle with half of the salt, pepper and bacon. Top with half of the sour cream and cheeses. Repeat layers.

2. Bake, uncovered, at 350° for 20 minutes or until cheese is melted. Sprinkle with onions. **Yield:** 6-8 servings.

Broccoli Rice Hot Dish —Gretchen Widner, Sun City West, Arizona

2 cups hot cooked rice
3/4 cup shredded reduced-fat cheddar cheese
1/2 cup egg substitute
3/4 teaspoon garlic salt
FILLING:
1 package (10 ounces) frozen chopped broccoli, thawed
4 ounces chopped fresh mushrooms
1/2 cup chopped sweet red pepper
1/2 medium onion, chopped
1 cup egg substitute
1/2 cup fat-free milk
1/2 teaspoon onion salt
1/2 teaspoon pepper
1 cup (4 ounces) shredded reduced-fat cheddar cheese

1. In a bowl, combine the rice, cheese, egg substitute and garlic salt. Press firmly into a 2-qt. baking dish coated with nonstick cooking spray. Bake at 375° for 10 minutes. Meanwhile, place the broccoli, mushrooms, red pepper and onion in a steamer basket over 1 in. of water in a saucepan. Bring to a boil; cover and steam for 5 minutes or until crisp-tender.

2. In a bowl, combine the egg substitute, milk, onion salt and pepper; stir in vegetables. Pour over crust. Sprinkle with cheese.

3. Bake, uncovered, at 375° for 25-30 minutes or until a knife inserted near the center comes out clean. **Yield:** 6 servings.

Reuben Casserole —Terri Holmgren, Swanville, Minnesota

1 can (14 ounces) sauerkraut, rinsed and drained
1 teaspoon caraway seeds
2 cups (8 ounces) shredded Monterey Jack *or* Swiss cheese, *divided*
1/2 cup Thousand Island salad dressing
1-1/4 cups cubed turkey pastrami
5 slices rye bread, cubed
1/3 cup butter, melted

1. Place the sauerkraut in a greased 2-qt. microwave-safe dish; sprinkle with caraway seeds and half of the cheese.

2. Top with the salad dressing, pastrami and remaining cheese. Toss bread cubes with butter; sprinkle over the top. Cover and microwave at 60% power for 8-10 minutes or until heated through. **Yield:** 4-6 servings.

Editor's Note: This recipe was tested in an 850-watt microwave.

Apple Pork Chop Casserole —Beverly Baxter, Kansas City, Kansas

2 boneless pork loin chops (3/4 inch thick)
2 teaspoons vegetable oil
3/4 cup water
1 tablespoon butter
1 small tart green apple, cored and chopped
2 tablespoons raisins
1-1/2 cups crushed chicken stuffing mix
2/3 cup condensed cream of mushroom soup, undiluted

1. In a skillet, brown meat in oil for about 5 minutes on each side. In a saucepan, combine the water, butter, apple and raisins; bring to a boil. Stir in stuffing mix. Remove from the heat; cover and let stand for 5 minutes. Fluff with fork.

2. Transfer to a greased shallow 1-qt. baking dish. Top with meat. Spoon soup over meat and stuffing. Cover and bake at 350° for 30-35 minutes or until a meat thermometer inserted into pork chops reads 160°. **Yield:** 2 servings.

Broccoli Rice Hot Dish

All-American Turkey Potpie –*Laureen Naylor, Factoryville, Pennsylvania*

2 cups all-purpose flour
1/2 teaspoon salt
1/2 cup finely shredded cheddar cheese
2/3 cup shortening
2 tablespoons cold butter
3 to 4 tablespoons cold water
FILLING:
1 cup diced peeled potatoes
1/2 cup thinly sliced carrots
1/3 cup chopped celery
1/4 cup chopped onion
1 garlic clove, minced
1 tablespoon butter
1 cup chicken *or* turkey broth
2 tablespoons all-purpose flour
1/2 cup milk
1-1/2 cups cubed cooked turkey
1/2 cup frozen peas, thawed
1/2 cup frozen corn, thawed
1/2 teaspoon salt
1/4 teaspoon dried tarragon
1/4 teaspoon pepper

1. In a food processor, combine flour and salt; cover and pulse to blend. Add cheese; pulse until fine crumbs form. Add shortening and butter; pulse until coarse crumbs form. Gradually add water until dough forms a ball. Divide dough in half with one ball slightly larger than the other; wrap in plastic wrap. Refrigerate for 30 minutes.

2. For filling, in a large saucepan, saute potatoes, carrots, celery, onion and garlic in butter for 5-6 minutes. Add broth; cover and cook for 10 minutes or until vegetables are tender. In a small bowl, combine flour and milk until smooth. Gradually add to vegetable mixture. Bring to a boil; cook and stir for 2 minutes or until thickened. Add the remaining ingredients; simmer 5 minutes longer.

3. Roll out larger pastry ball to fit a 9-in. pie plate; transfer to pie plate. Trim pastry even with edge. Pour hot turkey filling into crust. Roll out remaining pastry to fit top of pie; place over filling. Trim, seal and flute edges. Cut slits in top or make decorative cutouts in pastry.

4. Bake at 350° for 35-45 minutes or until crust is light golden brown. Serve immediately. **Yield:** 6-8 servings.

Cordon Bleu Casserole –*Joyce Paul, Moose Jaw, Saskatchewan*

4 cups cubed cooked turkey
3 cups cubed fully cooked ham
1 cup (4 ounces) shredded cheddar
   cheese
1 cup chopped onion
1/4 cup butter
1/3 cup all-purpose flour
2 cups half-and-half cream
1 teaspoon dill weed
1/8 teaspoon ground mustard
1/8 teaspoon ground nutmeg
TOPPING:
1 cup dry bread crumbs
2 tablespoons butter, melted
1/4 teaspoon dill weed
1/4 cup shredded cheddar cheese
1/4 cup chopped walnuts

1. In a large bowl, combine turkey, ham and cheese; set aside. In a saucepan, saute onion in butter until tender. Add flour; stir to form a paste. Gradually add cream, stirring constantly. Bring to a boil; boil 1 minute or until thick. Add dill, mustard and nutmeg; mix well. Remove from the heat and pour over meat mixture.

2. Spoon into a greased 13-in. x 9-in. x 2-in. baking dish. Toss bread crumbs, butter and dill; stir in cheese and walnuts. Sprinkle over the casserole. Bake, uncovered, at 350° for 30 minutes or until heated through. **Yield:** 8-10 servings.

Wild Rice Shrimp Bake –*Lee Stearns, Mobile, Alabama*

1 package (6 ounces) long grain and
   wild rice mix
1 pound uncooked medium shrimp,
   peeled and deveined
1 medium green pepper, chopped
1 medium onion, chopped
1 can (4 ounces) mushroom stems and
   pieces, drained
1/4 cup butter
1 can (10-3/4 ounces) condensed cream
   of chicken soup, undiluted
1/2 cup seasoned stuffing croutons

1. Prepare rice according to package directions. Meanwhile, in a large skillet, saute the shrimp, green pepper, onion and mushrooms in butter until shrimp turn pink. Add the soup to the rice; stir into the shrimp mixture.

2. Transfer to a greased 2-qt. baking dish. Sprinkle with croutons. Bake, uncovered, at 350° for 20-25 minutes or until heated through. **Yield:** 6 servings.

Chicken and Dumpling Casserole —Sue Mackey, Galesburg, Illinois

1/2 cup chopped onion
1/2 cup chopped celery
  2 garlic cloves, minced
1/4 cup butter
1/2 cup all-purpose flour
  2 teaspoons sugar
  1 teaspoon salt
  1 teaspoon dried basil
1/2 teaspoon pepper
  4 cups chicken broth
  1 package (10 ounces) frozen green peas
  4 cups cubed cooked chicken
DUMPLINGS:
  2 cups buttermilk biscuit mix
  2 teaspoons dried basil
2/3 cup milk

1. In a large saucepan, saute onion, celery and garlic in butter until tender. Add flour, sugar, salt, basil, pepper and broth; bring to a boil. Cook and stir for 1 minute; reduce heat. Add peas and cook for 5 minutes, stirring constantly. Stir in chick-en. Pour into a greased 13-in. x 9-in. x 2-in. baking dish.

2. For dumplings, combine biscuit mix and basil in a bowl. Stir in milk with a fork until moistened. Drop by tablespoonfuls onto casserole (12 dumplings).

3. Bake, uncovered, at 350° for 30 minutes. Cover and bake 10 minutes more or until dumplings are done. **Yield:** 6-8 servings.

Almond Turkey Casserole —Jill Black, Troy, Ontario

  2 cans (10-3/4 ounces *each*) condensed cream of mushroom soup, undiluted
1/2 cup mayonnaise
1/2 cup sour cream
  2 tablespoons chopped onion
  2 tablespoons lemon juice
  1 teaspoon salt
1/2 teaspoon white pepper
  5 cups cubed cooked turkey
  3 cups cooked rice
  4 celery ribs, chopped
  1 can (8 ounces) sliced water chestnuts, drained
  1 cup sliced almonds
TOPPING:
1-1/2 cups crushed butter-flavored crackers (about 38 crackers)
1/3 cup butter, melted
1/4 cup sliced almonds

1. In a large bowl, combine the soup, mayon-naise, sour cream, onion, lemon juice, salt and pepper. Stir in the turkey, rice, celery, water chestnuts and almonds. Transfer to a greased 13-in. x 9-in. x 2-in. baking dish.

2. Combine topping ingredients; sprinkle over turkey mixture. Bake, uncovered, at 350° for 35-40 minutes or until bubbly and golden brown. **Yield:** 8-10 servings.

Editor's Note: Reduced-fat or fat-free mayonnaise may not be substituted for regular mayonnaise.

Soups

Spinach Lentil Stew –*Alice McEachern, Surrey, British Columbia*

1/2 cup chopped onion
2 garlic cloves, minced
1 tablespoon canola oil
5 cups water
1 cup lentils, rinsed
4 teaspoons chicken bouillon granules
1 tablespoon Worcestershire sauce
1/2 teaspoon salt
1/2 teaspoon dried thyme
1/4 teaspoon pepper
1 bay leaf
1 cup chopped carrots
1 can (14-1/2 ounces) diced tomatoes, undrained

1 package (10 ounces) frozen chopped spinach, thawed and squeezed dry
1 tablespoon red wine vinegar

1. In a large saucepan, saute onion and garlic in oil until tender. Add the water, lentils, bouillon, Worcestershire sauce, salt, thyme, pepper and bay leaf; bring to a boil. Reduce heat; cover and simmer for 20 minutes.

2. Add carrots, tomatoes and spinach; return to a boil. Reduce heat; cover and simmer 15-20 minutes longer or until lentils are tender. Stir in vinegar. Discard bay leaf before serving. **Yield:** 6 servings.

Clam Chowder —*Melba Horne, Macon, Georgia*

6 bacon strips, diced
1/2 cup finely chopped onion
2 cans (10-3/4 ounces *each*) condensed cream of potato soup, undiluted
1-1/2 cups milk
3 cans (6-1/2 ounces *each*) minced clams, undrained
1 tablespoon lemon juice
1/4 teaspoon dried thyme
1/4 teaspoon pepper
Minced fresh parsley

1. In a large saucepan, cook bacon over medium heat until crisp; remove to paper towels. Drain, reserving 1 tablespoon drippings.

2. In the drippings, saute onion until tender. Stir in soup and milk. Add the clams, lemon juice, thyme, pepper and bacon; heat through. Garnish with parsley. **Yield:** 5 servings.

Stuffed Pepper Soup —*Hoss's Steak and Sea House, Meadville, Pennsylvania*

2 pounds ground beef
1 can (28 ounces) tomato sauce
1 can (28 ounces) diced tomatoes, undrained
2 cups cooked long grain white rice
2 cups chopped green pepper
2 beef bouillon cubes
1/4 cup packed brown sugar
2 teaspoons salt
1 teaspoon pepper

In a large saucepan or Dutch oven, cook beef over medium heat until no longer pink; drain. Add remaining ingredients; bring to a boil. Reduce heat; cover and simmer for 30-40 minutes or until peppers are tender. **Yield:** 10 servings.

Vegetable Beef Soup —*Agnes Bierbaum, Gainesville, Florida*

1/2 pound ground beef
2 cups water
1 can (14-1/2 ounces) stewed tomatoes
1 package (10 ounces) frozen mixed vegetables
1 can (8 ounces) tomato sauce
1 envelope onion soup mix
1/2 teaspoon sugar

In a saucepan, cook beef over medium heat until no longer pink; drain. Add the remaining ingredients; bring to a boil. Reduce heat; cover and simmer for 10-15 minutes or until the vegetables are tender. **Yield:** 6 servings.

Clam Chowder

White Bean 'n' Barley Soup *—Stephanie Land, Sudbury, Ontario*

1-1/2 cups dried great northern beans
   1 large onion, chopped
   2 garlic cloves, minced
   1 tablespoon olive oil
   4 cups chicken *or* vegetable broth
   4 cups water
   3 medium carrots, sliced
   2 medium sweet red peppers, diced
   2 celery ribs, chopped
1/2 cup medium pearl barley
1/2 cup minced fresh parsley, *divided*
   2 bay leaves
   1 teaspoon salt
1/2 teaspoon dried thyme

1/2 teaspoon pepper
   1 can (28 ounces) diced tomatoes, undrained

1. Place beans in a soup kettle or Dutch oven; add enough water to cover beans by 2 in. Bring to a boil; boil for 2 minutes. Remove from the heat; cover and let stand for 1-4 hours or until beans are softened.

2. Drain and rinse beans, discarding liquid. In a Dutch oven, saute onion and garlic in oil. Add the broth, water, beans, carrots, red peppers, celery, barley, 1/4 cup parsley, bay leaves, salt, thyme and pepper. Bring to a boil. Reduce heat; cover and simmer for 1 hour or until beans are tender. Add the tomatoes; heat through. Discard bay leaves. Sprinkle with remaining parsley. **Yield:** 9 servings.

Lemony Turkey Rice Soup –*Margarita Cuellar, East Chicago, Indiana*

     6 cups chicken broth, *divided*
     1 can (10-3/4 ounces) condensed cream
        of chicken soup, undiluted
     2 cups cooked rice
     2 cups diced cooked turkey
  1/4 teaspoon pepper
     2 tablespoons cornstarch
  1/4 to 1/3 cup lemon juice
  1/4 to 1/2 cup minced fresh cilantro

1. In a large saucepan, combine 5-1/2 cups broth, soup, rice, turkey and pepper. Bring to a boil; boil for 3 minutes.

2. In a small bowl, combine cornstarch and remaining broth until smooth. Gradually stir into hot soup. Cook and stir for 1-2 minutes or until thickened and heated through. Remove from the heat; stir in lemon juice and cilantro. **Yield:** 8 servings (about 2 quarts).

Hearty Cauliflower Soup –*Sarah Root, Twelve Mile, Indiana*

     4 cups cauliflowerets
     1 cup thinly sliced carrots
     2 cups water
     1 pound fully cooked smoked sausage,
        cubed
  1/2 cup chopped onion
  1/3 cup all-purpose flour
  3/4 teaspoon salt
  1/8 teaspoon pepper
     2 cups milk
     8 ounces process American cheese,
        cubed

1. In a saucepan, cook cauliflower and carrots in water until tender; set aside (do not drain). In a skillet over medium heat, cook the sausage and onion until sausage is browned; drain.

2. Add flour, salt and pepper; gradually add the milk. Bring to a boil; cook and stir for 2 minutes or until thickened. Add the reserved cauliflower, carrots and cooking liquid; heat through. Add cheese; stir until melted. **Yield:** 6-8 servings.

Broccoli Wild Rice Soup —*Martha Pollock, Oregonia, Ohio*

5 cups water
1 package (6 ounces) long grain and wild rice mix
1 can (10-3/4 ounces) reduced-fat reduced-sodium cream of chicken soup, undiluted
1-1/2 cups 1% milk
1 package (8 ounces) fat-free cream cheese, cubed
1/4 teaspoon salt
1 package (10 ounces) frozen chopped broccoli, thawed
1 large carrot, shredded
1/4 cup sliced almonds, toasted

1. In a large saucepan, combine the water and rice mix with contents of seasoning packet; bring to a boil. Reduce heat; cover and simmer for 20 minutes.

2. Add the soup, milk, cream cheese and salt; stir until cheese is melted. Add broccoli and carrot; cook over medium-low heat for 5-6 minutes or until vegetables and rice are tender. Garnish with almonds. **Yield:** 6 servings.

Editor's Note: This recipe was tested with Uncle Ben's Original Long Grain and Wild Rice Mix.

Texas Beef Stew —*Wilma James, Ranger, Texas*

1-1/4 pounds beef stew meat, cut into 1-inch pieces
1 to 2 tablespoons vegetable oil, optional
1/4 cup chopped onion
1-1/2 teaspoons garlic powder
1/4 teaspoon pepper
1 cup water
1 can (14-1/2 ounces) diced tomatoes, undrained
1 tablespoon ground cumin
1 teaspoon salt

1. In a large soup kettle or Dutch oven, brown beef, adding oil if desired; drain. Add onion, garlic powder, pepper and water; bring to a boil. Reduce heat; cover and simmer for 45 minutes or until meat is almost tender.

2. Add tomatoes, cumin and salt; return to a boil. Reduce heat; cover and simmer for 15-20 minutes or until meat is tender. **Yield:** 4 servings (1 quart).

Golden Squash Soup –*Mary Ann Klein, Washington Township, New Jersey*

3 leeks (white portion only), sliced
4 medium carrots, chopped
5 tablespoons butter
3 pounds butternut squash, peeled and cubed
6 cups chicken broth
3 medium zucchini, peeled and sliced
2 teaspoons salt
1/2 teaspoon dried thyme
1/4 teaspoon white pepper
1 cup half-and-half cream
1/2 cup milk
Grated Parmesan cheese and chives, optional

1. In a soup kettle or Dutch oven over medium heat, saute the leeks and carrots in butter for 5 minutes, stirring occasionally. Add squash, broth, zucchini, salt, thyme and pepper; bring to a boil. Reduce heat; cover and simmer until vegetables are tender, about 30 minutes. Cool until lukewarm.

2. In a blender or food processor, puree soup in small batches until smooth; return to kettle. Add cream and milk; mix well and heat through (do not boil). Garnish with Parmesan cheese and chives if desired. **Yield:** 12-14 servings (3-1/2 quarts).

Comforting Chicken Noodle Soup –*Joanna Sargent, Sandy, Utah*

2 quarts water
8 chicken bouillon cubes
6-1/2 cups uncooked wide egg noodles
2 cans (10-3/4 ounces *each*) condensed cream of chicken soup, undiluted
3 cups cubed cooked chicken
1 cup (8 ounces) sour cream
Minced fresh parsley

1. In a large saucepan, bring water and bouillon to a boil. Add noodles; cook, uncovered, until tender, about 10 minutes. Do not drain.

2. Add soup and chicken; heat through. Remove from the heat; stir in sour cream. Sprinkle with parsley. **Yield:** 10-12 servings (about 2-1/2 quarts).

Baked Potato Soup —*Loretha Bringle, Garland, Texas*

2/3 cup butter
2/3 cup all-purpose flour
7 cups milk
4 large baking potatoes, baked, cooled, peeled and cubed (about 4 cups)
4 green onions, sliced
12 bacon strips, cooked and crumbled
1-1/4 cups (5 ounces) shredded cheddar cheese
1 cup (8 ounces) sour cream
3/4 teaspoon salt
1/2 teaspoon pepper

1. In a large soup kettle or Dutch oven, melt the butter. Stir in flour until smooth; gradually add milk. Bring to a boil; cook and stir for 2 minutes or until thickened.

2. Add potatoes and onions. Bring to a boil, stirring constantly. Reduce heat; simmer for 10 minutes. Add remaining ingredients; stir until cheese is melted. Serve immediately. **Yield:** 8-10 servings (2-1/2 quarts).

Split Pea Soup —*Holly Dow, Chapman, Maine*

1 small onion, diced
1 tablespoon vegetable oil
4 cups water
1 can (14-1/2 ounces) chicken broth
1-1/2 cups dried split peas, rinsed
1 cup cubed fully cooked ham
3 bay leaves
1-1/2 teaspoons salt
1/2 teaspoon dried rosemary, crushed
1/4 teaspoon dried thyme
1/4 teaspoon pepper

In a large saucepan, saute onion in oil until tender. Add remaining ingredients. Bring to a boil; reduce heat. Cover and simmer for 1 hour or until peas are tender. Discard bay leaves. **Yield:** 6 servings.

Colby Corn Chowder —*Darlene Drane, Fayette, Missouri*

6 large potatoes, peeled and cubed
1 teaspoon salt
1 large onion, chopped
1/4 cup butter
2 cans (14-3/4 ounces *each*) cream-style corn
4 bacon strips, cooked and crumbled
3 cups milk
8 ounces Colby cheese, cubed

1. Place potatoes in a soup kettle or Dutch oven; sprinkle with salt and cover with water. Bring to a boil. Reduce heat; cover and simmer until potatoes are tender.

2. Meanwhile, in a skillet, saute onion in butter until tender. Stir in corn and bacon; heat through.

3. Drain potatoes; return to pan. Add milk; heat through. Stir in corn mixture and cheese; stir until cheese is melted. Serve immediately. **Yield:** 12-14 servings (about 3 quarts).

Snacks & Nibblers

Honey-Glazed Snack Mix –*Jan Olson, New Hope, Minnesota*

   8 **cups Crispix cereal**
   3 **cups miniature pretzels**
   2 **cups pecan halves**
2/3 **cup butter**
1/2 **cup honey**

1. In a large bowl, combine the cereal, pretzels and pecans; set aside. In a small saucepan, melt butter; stir in honey until well blended. Pour over cereal mixture and stir to coat.

2. Spread into two greased 15-in. x 10-in. x 1-in. baking pans. Bake at 350° for 12-15 minutes or until mixture is lightly glazed, stirring occasionally. Cool in pan for 3 minutes; remove from pan and spread on waxed paper to cool completely. Store in an airtight container. **Yield:** about 12 cups.

Spicy Barbecued Peanuts —*Linda Jonsson, Marion, Ohio*

1 egg white
2 tablespoons Liquid Smoke
3 cups salted peanuts
1/2 cup sugar
1 teaspoon chili powder
1 teaspoon ground cumin
1/4 teaspoon garlic powder
1/4 teaspoon cayenne pepper

1. In a bowl, whisk egg white until foamy. Add Liquid Smoke and peanuts; toss to coat. Combine the remaining ingredients. Sprinkle over nuts; toss to coat.

2. Spread in a single layer in a well-greased 15-in. x 10-in. x 1-in. baking pan. Bake at 250° for 1 hour, stirring once. Spread on waxed paper to cool. Store in an airtight container. **Yield:** 4-1/2 cups.

Sugared Curry Walnuts —*Ann Harris, Fresno, California*

1 tablespoon olive oil
1 teaspoon ground ginger
1 teaspoon curry powder
1/2 teaspoon cayenne pepper
1/4 cup sugar
2 tablespoons honey
3 cups walnut halves, toasted
1/2 teaspoon salt

1. In a large skillet, heat oil over medium heat. Stir in the ginger, curry powder and cayenne until smooth. Add sugar and honey; stir until blended. Stir in walnuts until well coated.

2. Spread onto a waxed paper-lined baking sheet. Sprinkle with salt. Cool and break apart. Store in an airtight container. **Yield:** 3 cups.

Parmesan-Garlic Popcorn –*Sharon Skildum, Maple Grove, Minnesota*

2-1/2 quarts popped popcorn, buttered
1/4 cup grated Parmesan cheese
1 teaspoon garlic powder
1 teaspoon dried parsley flakes
1/2 teaspoon dill weed

Place popcorn in a large bowl. In a small bowl, combine Parmesan cheese, garlic powder, parsley and dill; sprinkle over popcorn and toss lightly. Serve immediately. **Yield:** 2-1/2 quarts.

Crunchy Italian Mix –*Sharon Evans, Rockwell, Indiana*

1/2 cup butter
1 tablespoon Worcestershire sauce
1 teaspoon Italian seasoning
1/2 teaspoon garlic powder
5 cups Crispix cereal
2 cups Cheerios cereal
2-1/2 cups mini pretzels
1 can (10 ounces) mixed nuts
1/4 cup grated Parmesan cheese

1. In a saucepan or microwave-safe bowl, heat the first four ingredients until butter is melted; mix well. In a large bowl, combine the cereals, pretzels, nuts and Parmesan cheese. Drizzle with butter mixture and mix well. Place in an ungreased 15-in. x 10-in. x 1-in. baking pan.

2. Bake, uncovered, at 250° for 45 minutes, stirring every 15 minutes. Cool and store in an airtight container. **Yield:** 10 cups.

Crunchy Trail Mix —*Theresa Gingery, Holmesville, Nebraska*

1 package (16 ounces) milk chocolate
   M&M's
1 package (10 ounces) peanut butter
   chips
1 can (3 ounces) chow mein noodles
1-1/2 cups raisins
1-1/4 cups peanuts

In a large bowl, combine all ingredients; mix well. Store in an airtight container. **Yield:** 8 cups.

Corny Chocolate Crunch —*Delores Ward, Decatur, Indiana*

3 quarts popped popcorn
3 cups Corn Chex
3 cups broken corn chips
1 package (11 ounces)
   butterscotch chips
3/4 pound dark chocolate candy coating

1. In a large bowl, combine the popcorn, cereal and corn chips; set aside. In a saucepan over medium-low heat, melt butterscotch chips and candy coating; stir until smooth. Pour over popcorn mixture and toss to coat.

2. Spread into two greased 15-in. x 10-in. x 1-in. baking pans. When cool enough to handle, break into pieces. Store in an airtight container. **Yield:** about 5 quarts.

Golden Granola —*Maxine Smith, Owanka, South Dakota*

4 cups old-fashioned oats
1 cup flaked coconut
1/2 cup wheat germ
1/2 cup sesame seeds
1/2 cup sunflower seeds
1/2 cup slivered almonds
1-1/2 teaspoons salt
1-1/2 teaspoons ground cinnamon
1/2 cup vegetable oil
1/4 cup packed brown sugar
1/3 cup honey
1/3 cup water
1 tablespoon vanilla extract
1/2 cup golden raisins or chopped dried
   apricots

1. In a large bowl, combine the first eight ingredients; mix well. In a saucepan, cook oil, brown sugar, honey, water and vanilla until sugar is dissolved. Pour over dry ingredients and mix well. Spoon into a greased 13-in. x 9-in. x 2-in. baking pan.

2. Bake at 275° for 1 hour or until golden, stirring every 15 minutes. Cool completely. Stir in raisins or apricots. Store in an airtight container. **Yield:** about 9 cups.

Crunchy Trail Mix

Cinnamon Candy Popcorn —*Kay Kemper, Windfall, Indiana*

- **8 quarts plain popped popcorn**
- **1 cup butter**
- **1/2 cup light corn syrup**
- **1 package (9 ounces) red-hot candies**

1. Place popcorn in a large bowl and set aside. In a saucepan, combine butter, corn syrup and candies; bring to a boil over medium heat, stirring constantly. Boil for 5 minutes, stirring occasionally. Pour over popcorn and mix thoroughly. Turn into two greased 15-in. x 10-in. x 1-in. baking pans.

2. Bake at 250° for 1 hour, stirring every 15 minutes. Remove from pans and place on waxed paper to cool. Break apart; store in an airtight container. **Yield:** 8 quarts.

Cheesy Chive Crisps —*Eve McNew, St. Louis, Missouri*

- **1 cup butter, softened**
- **3 cups (12 ounces) shredded sharp cheddar cheese**
- **2 cups all-purpose flour**
- **1/4 cup minced chives**
- **1/2 teaspoon salt**
- **1/2 teaspoon hot pepper sauce**
- **Dash garlic salt**
- **2 cups crisp rice cereal**

1. In a large mixing bowl, cream butter and cheese until blended. Beat in the flour, chives, salt, hot pepper sauce and garlic salt. Stir in cereal. Shape into four 6-1/2-in. x 1-1/2-in. logs. Wrap in plastic wrap. Refrigerate for 1 hour or until firm.

2. Unwrap and cut into 1/4-in. slices. Place on ungreased baking sheets. Bake at 325° for 20-25 minutes or until edges are crisp and lightly browned. Remove to wire racks to cool. Store in the refrigerator or freezer. **Yield:** about 9 dozen.

Spicy Ribbon Potato Chips —*Sue Murphy, Greenwood, Michigan*

4 medium unpeeled baking potatoes
4 teaspoons salt, *divided*
4 cups ice water
1 tablespoon chili powder
1 teaspoon garlic salt
1/4 to 1/2 teaspoon cayenne pepper
Oil for deep-fat frying

1. Using a vegetable peeler or metal cheese slicer, cut potatoes into very thin lengthwise strips. Place in a large bowl; add 3 teaspoons salt and ice water. Soak for 30 minutes; drain.

2. Place potatoes on paper towels and pat dry. In a bowl, combine the chili powder, garlic salt, cayenne and remaining salt; set aside.

3. In an electric skillet or deep-fat fryer, heat oil to 375°. Cook potatoes in oil in batches for 3-4 minutes or until deep golden brown, stirring frequently. Remove with a slotted spoon; drain on paper towels. Immediately sprinkle with seasoning mixture. Store in an airtight container. **Yield:** 6-8 servings.

Cocoa Munch Mix —*Amanda Denton, Barre, Vermont*

4 cups Cheerios
4 cups Chex
1 cup slivered almonds
2 tablespoons baking cocoa
2 tablespoons sugar
1/2 cup butter, melted
1 cup raisins
1 package (12 ounces) vanilla *or* white chips

1. In a large bowl, combine the cereals and almonds. In a small bowl, combine cocoa, sugar and butter. Pour over cereal mixture and toss to coat. Pour into a greased 13-in. x 9-in. x 2-in. baking pan.

2. Bake at 250° for 1 hour, stirring every 15 minutes. Cool completely. Stir in raisins and chips. Store in an airtight container. **Yield:** 10 servings.

Cajun Party Mix —*Miriam Hershberger, Holmesville, Ohio*

2-1/2 cups Corn Chex cereal
2 cups Rice Chex cereal
2 cups Crispix cereal
1 cup mini pretzels
1 cup mixed nuts
1/2 cup butter, melted
1 tablespoon dried parsley flakes
1 teaspoon celery salt
1 teaspoon garlic powder
1/4 to 1/2 teaspoon cayenne pepper
1/4 teaspoon hot pepper sauce

1. Combine the cereals, pretzels and nuts. Pour into an ungreased 15-in. x 10-in. x 1-in. baking pan. Mix remaining ingredients; pour over the cereal mixture and stir to coat.

2. Bake at 250° for 40-60 minutes, stirring every 15 minutes. Cool and store in an airtight container. **Yield:** 8 cups.

Caramel Corn —*Nancy Breen, Canastota, New York*

12 quarts plain popped popcorn
1 pound peanuts
2 cups butter
2 pounds brown sugar
1/2 cup dark corn syrup
1/2 cup molasses

1. Place popcorn in two large bowls. Mix 1/2 pound nuts into each bowl. In a 5-qt. saucepan, combine remaining ingredients. Bring to a boil over medium heat; boil and stir for 5 minutes. Pour half of syrup over each bowl of popcorn and stir to coat. Turn coated popcorn into a large roasting pan.

2. Bake at 250° for 1 hour. Remove from the oven and break apart while warm. Cool. Store in an airtight container. **Yield:** 12 quarts.

Dips & Salsas

Five-Fruit Salsa —*Catherine Dawe, Kent, Ohio*

2 cups chopped fresh cantaloupe
6 green onions, chopped
3 kiwifruit, peeled and finely chopped
1 medium navel orange, peeled and finely chopped
1 medium sweet yellow pepper, chopped
1 medium sweet red pepper, chopped
1 can (8 ounces) crushed unsweetened pineapple, drained
2 jalapeno peppers, seeded and chopped
1 cup finely chopped fresh strawberries

CINNAMON TORTILLA CHIPS:
10 flour tortillas (8 inches)
1/4 cup butter, melted
1/3 cup sugar
2 teaspoons ground cinnamon

1. In a bowl, combine the first eight ingredients. Cover and refrigerate for 8 hours or overnight. Drain if desired. Just before serving, stir in strawberries.

2. For chips, brush tortillas with butter; cut each into eight wedges. Combine sugar and cinnamon; sprinkle over the tortillas. Place on ungreased baking sheets. Bake at 350° for 10-14 minutes or just until crisp. Serve with fruit salsa. **Yield:** 8 cups salsa and 80 chips.

Editor's Note: When cutting or seeding hot peppers, use rubber or plastic gloves to protect your hands. Avoid touching your face.

Summer Berry Salsa –Diane Hixon, Niceville, Florida

  1 pint fresh blueberries
  1 pint fresh strawberries, chopped
1/4 cup sugar
  2 tablespoons finely chopped onion
  1 tablespoon lemon juice
1/2 teaspoon pepper
  2 drops hot pepper sauce
1/4 cup slivered *or* sliced almonds,
     toasted

In a bowl, combine the first seven ingredients. Cover and refrigerate for 1 hour. Just before serving, stir in almonds. Serve with chicken, pork or fish. **Yield:** 4 cups.

Pretzel Mustard Dip –Bonnie Capper-Eckstein, Brooklyn Park, Minnesota

1/4 cup mayonnaise
1/4 cup prepared yellow *or* Dijon
     mustard
  2 tablespoons finely chopped onion
  1 tablespoon ranch salad dressing mix
2-1/4 teaspoons prepared horseradish
Pretzels

In a bowl, combine the mayonnaise, mustard, onion, salad dressing mix and horseradish. Cover and refrigerate for at least 30 minutes. Serve with pretzels. **Yield:** about 1/2 cup.

Taffy Apple Dip —Sue Gronholz, Columbus, Wisconsin

1 package (8 ounces) cream cheese, softened
3/4 cup packed brown sugar
1 tablespoon vanilla extract
1/2 cup chopped peanuts
6 medium apples, cut into wedges

In a small bowl, beat cream cheese, brown sugar and vanilla until smooth. Spread mixture on a small serving plate; top with nuts. Serve with apple wedges. **Yield:** 6 servings.

Four-Tomato Salsa —Connie Siese, Wayne, Michigan

7 plum tomatoes, chopped
7 medium tomatoes, chopped
3 medium yellow tomatoes, chopped
3 medium orange tomatoes, chopped
1 teaspoon salt
2 tablespoons lime juice
2 tablespoons olive oil
1 medium white onion, chopped
2/3 cup chopped red onion
2 green onions, chopped
1/2 cup *each* chopped sweet red, orange, yellow and green pepper
3 pepperoncinis, chopped
3 pickled sweet banana wax peppers, chopped
1/2 cup minced fresh parsley
2 tablespoons minced fresh cilantro
1 tablespoon dried chervil
Tortilla chips

In a colander, combine the tomatoes and salt. Let drain for 10 minutes. Transfer to a large bowl. Stir in the lime juice, oil, onions, peppers, parsley, cilantro and chervil. Serve with tortilla chips. Refrigerate or freeze leftovers. **Yield:** 14 cups.

Bacon Ranch Dip —*Pam Garwood, Lakeville, Minnesota*

1/2 cup mayonnaise
1/2 cup ranch salad dressing
1/2 cup sour cream
1/2 cup shredded Parmesan cheese
1/4 cup crumbled cooked bacon
Assorted fresh vegetables

In a bowl, combine the first five ingredients; mix well. Cover and refrigerate for at least 1 hour before serving. Serve with vegetables. **Yield:** 1-1/2 cups.

Cucumber Salsa —*Sandy Lee, Choctaw, Oklahoma*

2 medium cucumbers, peeled, seeded and chopped
2 medium tomatoes, chopped
1/2 cup chopped green pepper
1 jalapeno pepper, seeded and chopped
1 small onion, chopped
1 garlic clove, minced
2 tablespoons lime juice
1 teaspoon minced fresh parsley
2 teaspoons minced fresh cilantro
1/2 teaspoon dill weed
1/2 teaspoon salt
Tortilla chips

In a bowl, combine the first 11 ingredients. Cover and refrigerate for 1 hour. Serve with chips. **Yield:** 4 cups.

Editor's Note: When cutting or seeding hot peppers, use rubber or plastic gloves to protect your hands. Avoid touching your face.

Chunky Vegetable Dip —*Emma Magielda, Amsterdam, New York*

1 cup (8 ounces) sour cream
1/2 cup finely chopped seeded cucumber
1/4 cup chopped green onions
1/4 cup finely chopped radishes
1 to 2 tablespoons cider *or* tarragon vinegar
1-1/2 teaspoons prepared horseradish
3/4 teaspoon salt
1 large bell pepper, seeded and cut into a cup
Assorted fresh vegetables

In a bowl, combine the first seven ingredients; mix well. Cover and refrigerate. Serve in a pepper cup with vegetables for dipping. **Yield:** 1-1/2 cups.

Bacon Ranch Dip

Herbed Cheese Dip —*Patricia Kile, Greentown, Pennsylvania*

    1 package (8 ounces) cream cheese,
       softened
  1/4 cup milk
    1 tablespoon sour cream
    1 tablespoon minced fresh parsley
    1 teaspoon grated Parmesan cheese
    1 teaspoon olive oil
    1 teaspoon lemon juice
    1 teaspoon butter, softened
  3/4 teaspoon garlic powder
  1/2 teaspoon dried tarragon
  1/4 teaspoon celery seed
  1/8 teaspoon dill weed
Fresh vegetables

In a small mixing bowl, combine the first 12 ingredients; beat until smooth. Serve with vegetables. Store in the refrigerator. **Yield:** 1-1/2 cups.

Pineapple Mango Salsa —*Jeanne Wiestling, Minneapolis, Minnesota*

  1/4 cup diced fresh mango *or* peach
  1/4 cup canned pineapple chunks,
       quartered
    1 tablespoon finely chopped red onion
    1 teaspoon cider vinegar
  3/4 teaspoon minced fresh cilantro
  1/8 to 1/4 teaspoon ground ginger
Dash crushed red pepper flakes
Dash salt, optional
Tortilla chips

In a serving bowl, combine the mango, pineapple, red onion, vinegar, cilantro, ginger, pepper flakes and salt if desired. Cover and refrigerate for 1-4 hours. Stir before serving. Serve with tortilla chips. **Yield:** about 1/2 cup.

Mexican Fiesta Dip —Angela Oelschlaeger, Tonganoxie, Kansas

    1 pound lean ground turkey
    1 envelope taco seasoning
  2/3 cup water
    1 can (16 ounces) refried beans
1-1/2 cups shredded lettuce
    1 jar (16 ounces) salsa
    1 cup (4 ounces) shredded cheddar
      cheese
    4 canned jalapenos, sliced
    1 cup (8 ounces) sour cream
  1/3 cup sliced ripe olives
    1 package (13-1/2 ounces) tortilla chips

1. In a nonstick skillet coated with nonstick cooking spray, cook turkey until no longer pink; drain if necessary. Stir in taco seasoning and water; cook and stir for 2-4 minutes or until most of the liquid has evaporated.

2. Spread refried beans on a 12-in. serving platter. Top with the turkey, lettuce, salsa, cheese, jalapenos, sour cream and olives. Serve with chips. **Yield:** 12 servings

Calico Cheese Dip —Ellen Keck, Granger, Indiana

    4 cups (16 ounces) shredded Monterey
      Jack cheese
    1 can (4 ounces) chopped green chilies
    1 can (2-1/4 ounces) sliced ripe olives,
      drained
    4 green onions, sliced
    3 medium tomatoes, seeded and diced
  1/2 cup minced fresh parsley
    1 envelope Italian salad dressing mix
Tortilla chips

In a mixing bowl, combine the cheese, chilies, olives, onions, tomatoes and parsley. Prepare salad dressing mix according to package directions; pour over cheese mixture and mix well. Serve immediately with tortilla chips. **Yield:** 6 cups.

Tropical Fruit Dip *–Suzanne Strocsher, Bothell, Washington*

1 carton (16 ounces) cottage cheese
1/4 cup lemon yogurt *or* flavor of your
    choice
3 to 4 tablespoons honey
1 teaspoon grated orange peel
2 tablespoons flaked coconut, toasted
Assorted fresh fruit

Place the cottage cheese and yogurt in a blender; cover and process until smooth. Stir in honey and orange peel. Pour into a serving dish. Cover and refrigerate for at least 1 hour. Sprinkle with coconut. Serve with fruit. **Yield:** about 1-1/2 cups.

Creamy Swiss Spinach Dip *–Heather Millican, Fort Meyers, Florida*

1 package (8 ounces) cream cheese,
    softened
1 teaspoon garlic powder
1 package (9 ounces) frozen creamed
    spinach, thawed
2 cups diced Swiss cheese
2 unsliced round loaves (1 pound *each*)
    Italian *or* French bread

1. In a small microwave-safe mixing bowl, beat cream cheese and garlic powder until smooth. Stir in spinach and Swiss cheese. Cover and microwave on high for 5-8 minutes or until cheese is melted, stirring occasionally.

2. Meanwhile, cut a 4-in. circle in the center of one loaf of bread. Remove bread, leaving 1 in. at bottom of loaf. Cut removed bread and the second loaf into 1-1/2-in. cubes. Spoon hot spinach

dip into bread shell. Serve with bread cubes. **Yield:** 3-1/2 cups.

    Editor's Note: This recipe was tested in an 850-watt microwave.

Cinnamon 'n' Spice Dip *–Julie Bertha, Pittsburgh, Pennsylvania*

2 cups whipped topping
1/4 cup packed brown sugar
1/8 to 1/4 teaspoon ground cinnamon
Dash ground nutmeg
Assorted fresh fruit

In a small bowl, combine the whipped topping, brown sugar, cinnamon and nutmeg. Serve with fruit. **Yield:** about 2 cups.

Condiments

Spicy Mustard —*Joyce Lonsdale, Unionville, Pennsylvania*

- 1/2 cup tarragon *or* cider vinegar
- 1/2 cup water
- 1/4 cup olive oil
- 2 tablespoons prepared horseradish
- 1/2 teaspoon lemon juice
- 1 cup ground mustard
- 1/2 cup sugar
- 1/2 teaspoon salt

1. In a blender or food processor, combine all ingredients. Process for 1 minute. Scrape down the sides of the container and process for 30 seconds. Transfer to a small saucepan and let stand 10 minutes.

2. Cook over low heat, stirring constantly, until bubbly. Cool completely. If a thinner mustard is desired, stir in an additional 1-2 tablespoons water. Pour into small containers with tight-fitting lids. Store in the refrigerator. **Yield:** 1-1/2 cups.

Creole Seasoning Mix —*Marion Platt, Sequim, Washington*

2 tablespoons plus 1-1/2 teaspoons
  paprika
2 tablespoons garlic powder
1 tablespoon salt
1 tablespoon onion powder
1 tablespoon dried oregano
1 tablespoon dried thyme
1 tablespoon cayenne pepper
1 tablespoon pepper

Combine all ingredients. Store in an airtight container. Use to season chicken, seafood, steaks or vegetables. **Yield:** 1 batch (about 1/2 cup).

Orange-Caramel Ice Cream Sauce —*Taste of Home Test Kitchen*

1 cup packed brown sugar
1 cup heavy whipping cream
1/2 cup sweetened condensed milk
1/2 teaspoon orange extract
Butter pecan ice cream
Orange spirals, optional

1. In a saucepan, cook and stir brown sugar and cream over medium heat until sugar is dissolved. Bring to a boil; cook for 5 minutes or until mixture is reduced by half. Remove from the heat.

2. Stir in milk and orange extract. Cover and refrigerate. Just before serving, warm over low heat. Serve over ice cream. Garnish with orange spirals if desired. **Yield:** 1-1/3 cups.

Freezer Cucumber Pickles —*Connie Goense, Pembroke Pine, Florida*

    4 pounds pickling cucumbers, sliced
    8 cups thinly sliced onions
  1/4 cup salt
  3/4 cup water
    4 cups sugar
    2 cups cider vinegar

1. Combine cucumbers, onions, salt and water in two large bowls. Let stand at room temperature for 2 hours.

2. Add sugar and vinegar; stir until sugar dissolves. Pack into 1-pint freezer containers, leaving 1-in. headspace. Cover and freeze for up to 6 weeks. Thaw at room temperature for 4 hours before serving. **Yield:** 10 pints.

Texas Jalapeno Jelly —*Lori McMullen, Victoria, Texas*

    2 jalapeno peppers, seeded and
      chopped
    3 medium green peppers, cut into
      1-inch pieces, *divided*
1-1/2 cups vinegar, *divided*
6-1/2 cups sugar
  1/2 to 1 teaspoon cayenne pepper
    2 pouches (3 ounces *each*) liquid fruit
      pectin
About 6 drops green food coloring, optional
Cream cheese and crackers, optional

1. In a blender or food processor, place the jalapenos, half of the green peppers and 1/2 cup vinegar; cover and process until pureed.

2. Transfer to a Dutch oven or large kettle. Repeat with remaining green peppers and another 1/2 cup vinegar. Add sugar, cayenne and remaining vinegar to the pan.

3. Bring to a rolling boil over high heat, stirring constantly. Quickly stir in pectin and return to a

rolling boil. Boil for 1 minute, stirring constantly. Remove from the heat; skim off foam. Add food coloring if desired.

4. Ladle hot liquid into hot jars, leaving 1/4-in. headspace. Cover with lids. Process for 10 minutes in a boiling-water bath. Serve over cream cheese with crackers if desired. **Yield:** 7 half-pints.

Cinnamon Apple Jelly —*Virginia Montmarquet, Riverside, California*

7 cups unsweetened bottled apple juice
1 package (1-3/4 ounces) powdered
    fruit pectin
2 teaspoons butter
1 cup red-hot candies
9 cups sugar

1. Place the apple juice in a large kettle. Stir in pectin and butter. Bring to a full rolling boil over high heat, stirring constantly. Stir in candies until dissolved. Stir in sugar; return to a full rolling boil. Boil for 1 minute, stirring constantly. Remove from the heat; skim off foam.

2. Pour hot mixture into hot sterilized jars, leaving 1/4-in. headspace. Adjust caps. Process for 5 minutes in a boiling-water bath. **Yield:** about 13 half-pints.

Peanut Butter Spread —*Maudie Raber, Millersburg, Ohio*

2 cups peanut butter
1 jar (7 ounces) marshmallow creme
1 cup dark corn syrup
1 cup light corn syrup

In a mixing bowl, combine all ingredients; mix well. Place in sterilized half-pint jars. Store at room temperature. **Yield:** 5 half-pints.

Left to right: Peanut Butter Spread, Cinnamon Apple Jelly

Dill Mustard —*Sue Braunschweig, Delafield, Wisconsin*

1 cup ground mustard
1 cup cider vinegar
3/4 cup sugar
1/4 cup water
2 teaspoons salt
1-1/2 teaspoons dill weed
2 eggs, lightly beaten

In the top of a double boiler, combine mustard, vinegar, sugar, water, salt and dill. Cover and let stand at room temperature for 4 hours. Bring water in bottom of double boiler to a boil. Add eggs to mustard mixture. Cook and stir until thickened, about 10 minutes. Cool. Store in refrigerator. **Yield:** about 2 cups.

Chunky Peach Spread —*Rebecca Baird, Salt Lake City, Utah*

7 medium peaches (2 to 2-1/2 pounds)
1/3 cup sugar
1 tablespoon lemon juice
1 envelope unflavored gelatin
1/4 cup cold water

1. Drop peaches in boiling water for 1 minute or until peel has softened. Immediately dip fruit in ice water. Peel and chop peaches. In a large saucepan, combine the peaches, sugar and lemon juice. Bring to a boil. Mash peaches. Reduce heat; simmer, uncovered, for 5 minutes.

2. Meanwhile, in a small bowl, sprinkle gelatin over cold water; let stand for 2 minutes. Remove peach mixture from the heat; stir in gelatin mixture until dissolved. Cool for 10 minutes. Pour into jars. Refrigerate for up to 3 weeks. **Yield:** about 3-1/2 cups.

Mediterranean Herb Rub —*Jacqueline Thompson Graves, Lawrenceville, Georgia*

1 tablespoon dried thyme
1 tablespoon dried oregano
1-1/2 teaspoons poultry seasoning
1 teaspoon dried rosemary, crushed
1 teaspoon dried marjoram
1 teaspoon dried basil
1 teaspoon dried parsley flakes
1/8 teaspoon pepper

In a small bowl, combine all ingredients. Store in an airtight container in a cool dry place for up to 6 months. **Yield:** 1/4 cup.

Freezer Salsa Jam –Ellen Katzke, Delavan, Minnesota

2 cups finely chopped plum tomatoes
  (6 to 7)
1/2 cup finely chopped onion
1 can (8 ounces) tomato sauce
1/4 cup chopped fresh cilantro
1/4 cup finely chopped fresh *or* canned
  jalapeno peppers
2 tablespoons lime juice
1 teaspoon grated lime peel
1/4 teaspoon hot pepper sauce
1-1/2 cups sugar
1 package (1-3/4 ounces) of
  powdered pectin for low sugar recipes
  (no substitutes)
1/4 cup water

1. In a large bowl, combine the tomatoes, onion, tomato sauce, cilantro, peppers, lime juice, peel and hot pepper sauce; set aside.

2. In a large saucepan, combine sugar and pectin; stir in water. Bring to a boil; boil and stir for 1 minute. Remove from the heat. Stir into tomato mixture; continue to stir until well combined.

3. Pour into jars or plastic containers. Cover and let stand overnight or until set, but not longer than 24 hours. Regrigerate for up to 3 weeks or freeze for up to 1 year. **Yield:** 4-1/2 cups.

Chunky Fruit and Nut Relish –Donna Brockett, Kingfisher, Oklahoma

2 packages (12 ounces *each*) fresh *or*
  frozen cranberries
1-1/2 cups sugar
1 cup orange juice
1 can (16 ounces) sliced peaches,
  drained and cut up
1 can (8 ounces) pineapple tidbits,
  drained
1 cup chopped pecans
1/2 cup golden raisins

1. In a large saucepan, bring cranberries, sugar and orange juice to a boil, stirring occasionally. Reduce heat and simmer, uncovered, for 8-10 minutes or until the berries burst.

2. Remove from the heat; stir in peaches, pineapple, pecans and raisins. Cool. Cover and refrigerate at least 3 hours. **Yield:** about 6 cups.

Lemonade Fruit Dressing –Emma Magielda, Amsterdam, New York

2 eggs
3/4 cup lemonade concentrate
1/3 cup sugar
1 cup heavy whipping cream, whipped
Assorted fresh fruit

1. In a heavy saucepan, combine eggs, lemonade concentrate and sugar. Cook and stir over low heat just until mixture comes to a boil.

2. Cool to room temperature, stirring several times. Fold in the whipped cream. Serve over fruit. Refrigerate leftovers. **Yield:** about 3 cups.

Rosemary Jelly –Margaret Dumire, Carroll, Ohio

1-1/4 cups boiling water
2 tablespoons minced fresh rosemary
3 cups sugar
1/4 cup vinegar
1 pouch (3 ounces) liquid fruit pectin
2 to 3 drops green food coloring

1. In a large saucepan, combine boiling water and rosemary; cover and let stand for 15 minutes. Strain, reserving liquid. If necessary, add water to measure 1-1/4 cups. Return liquid to pan; add sugar and vinegar. Bring to a full rolling boil over high heat, stirring constantly. Add pectin, stirring until mixture boils. Boil and stir for 1 minute.

2. Remove from the heat; skim off foam. Add food coloring if desired. Pour hot mixture into hot jars, leaving 1/4-in. headspace. Adjust caps. Process for 10 minutes in a boiling-water bath. **Yield:** 3-1/2 pints.

Orange Pear Jam –Delores Ward, Decatur, Indiana

7 cups sugar
5 cups chopped peeled fresh pears
1 cup crushed pineapple, drained
2 tablespoons lemon juice
2 packages (3 ounces *each*) orange gelatin

1. In a Dutch oven or large kettle, combine the sugar, pears, pineapple and lemon juice. Bring to a full rolling boil over high heat, stirring constantly. Reduce heat; simmer for 15 minutes, stirring frequently. Remove from the heat; stir in gelatin until dissolved.

2. Pour into jars or containers; cool to room temperature, about 1 hour. Cover and let stand overnight or until set, but not longer than 24 hours. Refrigerate for up to 3 weeks. **Yield:** about 7 cups.

General Index

Alphabetical Index

A

B

C

Substitutions & Equivalents

Equivalent Measures

3 teaspoons	=	1 tablespoon	16 tablespoons	=	1 cup
4 tablespoons	=	1/4 cup	2 cups	=	1 pint
5-1/3 tablespoons	=	1/3 cup	4 cups	=	1 quart
8 tablespoons	=	1/2 cup	4 quarts	=	1 gallon

Food Equivalents

Grains

Macaroni	1 cup (3-1/2 ounces) uncooked	=	2-1/2 cups cooked
Noodles, Medium	3 cups (4 ounces) uncooked	=	4 cups cooked
Popcorn	1/3 to 1/2 cup unpopped	=	8 cups popped
Rice, Long Grain	1 cup uncooked	=	3 cups cooked
Rice, Quick-Cooking	1 cup uncooked	=	2 cups cooked
Spaghetti	8 ounces uncooked	=	4 cups cooked

Crumbs

Bread	1 slice	=	3/4 cup soft crumbs, 1/4 cup fine dry crumbs
Graham Crackers	7 squares	=	1/2 cup finely crushed
Buttery Round Crackers	12 crackers	=	1/2 cup finely crushed
Saltine Crackers	14 crackers	=	1/2 cup finely crushed

Fruits

Bananas	1 medium	=	1/3 cup mashed
Lemons	1 medium	=	3 tablespoons juice, 2 teaspoons grated peel
Limes	1 medium	=	2 tablespoons juice, 1-1/2 teaspoons grated peel
Oranges	1 medium	=	1/4 to 1/3 cup juice, 4 teaspoons grated peel

Vegetables

Cabbage	1 head	=	5 cups shredded	Green Pepper	1 large	=	1 cup chopped
Carrots	1 pound	=	3 cups shredded	Mushrooms	1/2 pound	=	3 cups sliced
Celery	1 rib	=	1/2 cup chopped	Onions	1 medium	=	1/2 cup chopped
Corn	1 ear fresh	=	2/3 cup kernels	Potatoes	3 medium	=	2 cups cubed

Nuts

Almonds	1 pound	=	3 cups chopped	Pecan Halves	1 pound	=	4-1/2 cups chopped
Ground Nuts	3-3/4 ounces	=	1 cup	Walnuts	1 pound	=	3-3/4 cups chopped

Easy Substitutions

When you need...		Use...
Baking Powder	1 teaspoon	1/2 teaspoon cream of tartar + 1/4 teaspoon baking soda
Buttermilk	1 cup	1 tablespoon lemon juice *or* vinegar + enough milk to measure 1 cup (let stand 5 minutes before using)
Cornstarch	1 tablespoon	2 tablespoons all-purpose flour
Honey	1 cup	1-1/4 cups sugar + 1/4 cup water
Half-and-Half Cream	1 cup	1 tablespoon melted butter + enough whole milk to measure 1 cup
Onion	1 small, chopped (1/3 cup)	1 teaspoon onion powder *or* 1 tablespoon dried minced onion
Tomato Juice	1 cup	1/2 cup tomato sauce + 1/2 cup water
Tomato Sauce	2 cups	3/4 cup tomato paste + 1 cup water
Unsweetened Chocolate	1 square (1 ounce)	3 tablespoons baking cocoa + 1 tablespoon shortening *or* oil
Whole Milk	1 cup	1/2 cup evaporated milk + 1/2 cup water

Gifts from the Country Kitchen